Joinings, Edges, and Trims

Finishing Details for Handcrafted Products

Jean Wilson

VNR **VAN NOSTRAND REINHOLD COMPANY**
New York Cincinnati Toronto London Melbourne

Acknowledgments

My deepest and continuing appreciation to all of you enthusiastic weavers and embroiderers who have come to my workshops and slide/lectures and still wanted more!

To members of my Seattle Weavers' Guild for continuing interest and use of total design in completely handcrafted products.

To good friends like Virginia Isham Harvey, Anita Mayer, Leslie Grace, Beverly Rush, Sylvia and Harold Tacker, and so many others who are always ready to try ideas, provide material for study, and unfailing reinforcement.

To Jill Nordfors and Jane McClenney for their excellent drawings, which are so important.

To all who shared their work with me.

To Irene Demchyshyn, for understanding, and her wise and patient editing of this complex subject.

And, as always, to my husband Ron, who photographed, advised, and is so supportive of my efforts.

Printed in the United States of America
Designed by Loudan Enterprises

Published by Van Nostrand Reinhold Company Inc.
135 West 50th Street, New York, NY 10020

Van Nostrand Reinhold
480 Latrobe Street
Melbourne, Victoria 3000, Australia

Van Nostrand Reinhold Company Limited
Molly Millars Lane
Wokingham, Berkshire, England RG11 2PY

16 15 14 13 12 11 10 9 8 7 6 5 4 3 2 1

Library of Congress Cataloging in Publication Data
Wilson, Jean Verseput.
Joinings, edges, and trims.

Bibliography: p.
Includes index.
1. Hand weaving. 2. Embroidery. 3. Borders, Ornamental.
4. Seams (Sewing) I. Title.
TT848.W478   746.1′4   82-4857
ISBN 0-442-29538-3   AACR2

Drawings by Jane McClenney: 2-8, 2-11, 2-14, 2-15, 2-24, 2-26, 2-39, 2-57, 2-62, 2-68, 3-37, 3-43, 3-53, 3-54, 3-70, 4-25. Drawings by Jill Nordfors: 3-20, 3-22, 3-23, 3-24, 3-28, 3-30, 3-32, 3-35, 3-36, 3-40, 3-45, 3-47. All of the warp-end finishes were drawn by Gary Wilson. Unless otherwise noted, all photographs are by Ron Wilson. Unless otherwise noted, all examples by the author.

Contents

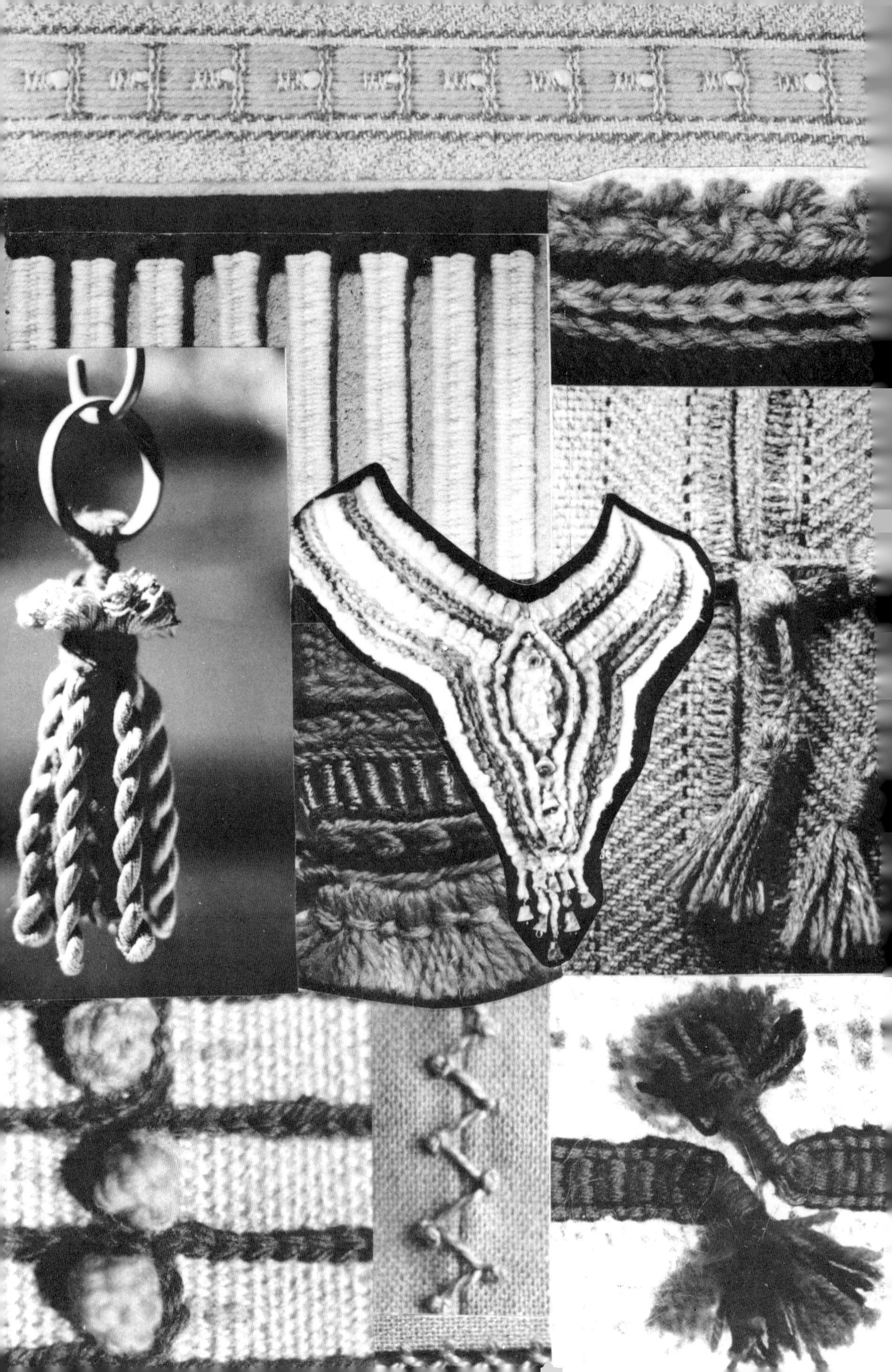

Preface

This book is offered as a guide to ways of finishing textiles and to the equally important planning of a total design: how to approach and complete a weaving project, with examples, directions, references, and options. Extend the use of your loom by doing some of the finishing on the loom. Exact techniques are given, but I definitely urge you to try everything you can think of. Freely experiment, with no set plan or specific use, and see where the limitations and expansion of a technique lead you.

The need for planning ahead and conceiving your total design, however, becomes very apparent the moment you sit before an empty warp, ready to work the first technique. Planning should come even before that so that you can select the right warp, sett, color, and perhaps the type of loom to use.

There is no single *best* way to sew a hem, close a seam, or fashion a tassel. Usually, however, there is a best way to treat a specific need. Weaving an idea takes longer than writing about one, but try enough on a sampling loom or cloth to see what works, and explore variations and adaptations of weaves and stitches. When you look at your weaving with the idea of finishing as much as possible on the loom, as you progress you will see more and more possibilities: working embroidery stitches along an edge that is to become a part of a join, for example. It is so easy to do while the whole thing is in tension.

Some study sources are available and mentioned—there for your discovery. Some design sources and a selected bibliography are included as well. I have tried to open to you some of the doors behind which I have found richness and knowledge. These techniques and suggestions apply to almost any textile project and should help you to plan and complete wearable, household, or decorative textiles.

Assembled trims, tassel closures, and embellishments. (Button and cord closure, also shown in figure 5-22, by Jan Burhen; band and tassel trim by Lucy Driver; joining embroidery stitches by Beverly Rush; other examples by the author)

Introduction

Every piece of cloth has four edges: two warp ends and two selvedges. The first and major concern at the warp ends is to protect the weft from becoming unwoven when the textile is cut from the loom. Weaving neat, straight, firm selvedges is another important concern, whether they are to be left as is, or become a part of a joining, or be otherwise embellished. Beyond the basic considerations and decisions for the proper and suitable finishing of the four edges, a whole world of possibilities opens up; it is limited only by the intended use of the loom product, practicality, and judicious use of enrichment. The methods and techniques, ideas, and examples that will be discussed apply to all products of your loom and needle, whether for clothing, household textiles, or decorative pieces.

This book is designed to give you dozens of ideas—some design sources, some exact techniques—and suggestions for experimentation, but I sincerely urge you to try ideas of your own. Toss every idea about and come up with new and fresh approaches. When exploring a technique, approach it with no set plan, maybe not even thinking of the ultimate use. Just play with it and see what it will do for you. Then you will be ready to bring a wealth of ideas and skill to the careful planning of a specific work.

ARRANGEMENT OF SUBJECTS

A textile is woven. Warp and weft combine to make a selvedge. Selvedges are joined with an embroidery stitch. The embroidery stitch is expanded into a band and becomes a trim. A trim is enhanced with more stitches, tassels, or fringe and becomes an embellishment.

When does an edge preparation for a joining, joined with a showy stitch, become a trim? When is it just a join?

On the loom, a firmly woven, even selvedge is given a row of buttonhole needle stitches, which is part of a join. Off the loom, two sections are joined with a lacing stitch. A row or two of a decorative needle stitch may be added along each side of the seam.

A hem is turned up onto the right side of the cloth. It is sewn with a row of closed herringbone stitch and becomes a trim instead of just a hem.

Chained rows are woven in with the loops at

A montage of ideas and techniques: fastfringe, five-strand join, tied join, neckline reinforcement, and embroidery stitches.

the edge for buttonholes. Handmade buttons are added. This is a trimming—and a closure.

An edge finish is woven on. The pattern, colors, and textures are a trim.

A weft fringe is an extension from the selvedge and may be part of a tied join.

So you see that a neat, categorized arrangement of subjects is not easy—or even feasible. Major headings and cross-references will help you locate techniques.

Be forewarned! Many of these special touches, weaver-controlled techniques, and hand methods are time consuming, but they are worth the time and extra effort for your unique handcrafted result. Handstitching is a greedy consumer of time. It actually does take hours, but this time is used to a good purpose and a carefully planned handwoven article deserves an equally well-planned finish. Admonitions, precautions, suggestions—and warnings—have evolved through my own trials and errors and experience, so they are passed along to you for whatever help they may provide.

Variables in working with fibers are ever-present and, even with precise rules to follow, you still have to improvise and change to fit your particular materials and design. This is part of the exciting challenge and points up the need for a fund of techniques, methods, and references. Don't settle for the first try; keep on experimenting and sampling, enlarging your understanding and knowledge.

MY CREED—PASSED ALONG TO YOU

- Think total design.
- Learn all of the techniques and methods, both on the loom and on the textile off the loom, for a rich store to draw from.
- Constantly make examples for learning, experience, and reference. Even a small sampling will be of value. The idea will be there to see.
- Try every variation, trial and error method, that you can think of. No matter that you take out more than you put in! Better here than directly on your production.
- When you weave a sample for testing of washing and shrinkage, weave enough to try some finishing methods, too. This is particularly important for clothing, but it is helpful for household weavings, too. Then, on the exact cloth,

you can try the hem, seam, or special stitch and thread to be used.
- Always keep in mind suitability of purpose, use, practicality, and aesthetics. These must be balanced in your total design, from the type of loom used, through warp and weft choices, color, and sett, to the exact stitch and kind of hem, join, or trim.

WORKSHOPS

For those of you who may not have the opportunity to attend workshops, are teaching and need some hints, or belong to small groups helping each other, chapter 1 details some of my methods and teaching aids developed over several years of teaching. Even if you are on your own, this might help you to organize your own learning process.

Ideas, methods, techniques, materials—all these have to come from somewhere! In our day, with thousands of years of textile and fiber experience behind us, we have an abundance of reference material. It follows that more and more analysis, findings, writings, and teachings are offered to the ever-growing numbers of students and fabricators of textiles. Much of the easily accessible material has been studied exhaustively. Much is still to be done, and discovery goes on.

PLANNING AND TOTAL DESIGN

'Plan Ahead' is the watchword and key to a complete, handcrafted product that you can be proud of, whether you weave it to shape and size, cut and sew, or work with ready-woven fabric. For a weaver, planning means that you start with the selection of the loom best suited to your purpose—after the product is designed. Then, choices are made for warp, sett, weft, techniques, method of production, finishing with machine sewing or handwork, fabrication, and assembly.

Compose Your Complete Weaving

Thinking through a whole project from start to finish is the important first step, especially for a weaver. Planning is critical when a particular effect is desired or if certain preliminary steps must be taken. For example, if the woven piece will have a warp fringe, the warp is chosen for the right color, the right size and spin, and the right fiber (one that will wear well with cut ends). Or, a join may be planned that requires special warping at the selvedge and some extra methods used in the weaving. If you want loop warp ends, your decisions will start with the choice of loom to be used—either a backstrap or a stretcher-frame loom warped so the frame can be slipped out, leaving loops.

Think of surface textures and contrast as well as color. A yarn may have no sheen; a mercerized thread will have some gloss; a metal button may have a satin finish or high polish. Yarn may be smooth, plied, thick and thin spin, or nubby. All of these factors will be emphasized or minimized by the lighting, movement, and surface textures woven or embroidered.

The view from the back is important, too, especially if it is to be seen, as in a room divider, an unlined jacket, a table napkin, or a scarf. Tidy it up by disposing of weft ends during the weaving, or later. Hide beginnings and ends of embroidery stitches within the stitch and make sure that hems and seams look neat from either side.

Happenings are fun—and it is good to have some leeway for a change of plan when a smashing idea comes midway in the weaving. Some of the most exciting and best products are the result of some special effect that "just happened" when yarns and methods came together. Some projects should certainly be approached with an open mind and experimenting fingers.

Careful planning is another way to create and is essential for weavings that need to be precise in measurement and completely right for a specific purpose. However, if finishing problems are afterthoughts, there is usually a way of solving them attractively, and some of my suggestions may help there.

That Extra Touch

In handcrafts—weaving and embroidery—some important considerations should be kept foremost in mind:

- Know when to stop embellishing! Restrict yourself to selected colors, yarns, and techniques. For a sophisticated result, use restraint.
- Subtle effects do not have to be dull!
- The components should be completely compatible in materials, techniques, and methods.
- Guard against becoming so intrigued with a color or combination of colors that you forget to notice textures and the surface effect of the spin of the yarn, the scale, the sheen, and the changing light. These factors are all a part of the whole composition.

Sources of Design, Ideas, and Study

There are many conventional ways to stitch and seam with a sewing machine; our theme is not only to reach beyond this, to utilize alternate methods and handwork, especially on your own handwoven textile, but also to bring creative handwork to commercial fabrics.

Whether you dip into pages on specific techniques when you need a closure or a fringe idea, or follow the reference/sampler suggestions, this text should bring an awareness of scope and how to achieve appropriate finishes and trims. The more you do, the more ideas you will have as adaptations and variations present themselves with each specific solution. Just changing a color or size of yarn will alter the look and use of a stitch or weave.

Use this as a springboard for your own designing. It has been difficult to corral this material and cram it between two covers! Each idea multiplied and grew until choices and time to fabricate them became a real challenge.

1. Reference/Samplers

After several years of teaching and writing about the extensive subject of joinings, trims, edges, and finishes, I have some suggestions about how you might approach learning and employing these techniques. After you have planned and designed a piece, there are two phases: what can be done on the loom; and what can be done with the cloth, off from the loom.

A woven scroll of techniques and ideas; a reference/sampler of stitches; edges, and joins on cloth; and working variations of a few stitches on cloth in embroidery hoops are teaching aids I have devised to teach Phase I, on the loom, and Phase II, off the loom. They are shown here, with brief identifying descriptions. Directions and more examples are found in succeeding chapters. If you choose to learn these methods this workshop way, you will have a fund of techniques to draw from when needed for a specific product.

PHASE I

In Phase I you learn what must be done in the planning of a project and what part can best be worked on the loom. I suggest that you weave a reference/sampler similar to the scroll shown in figure 1-1. This is an excellent way to try out new methods, techniques, variations, and adaptations. Sampling is never a waste of time because it is part of your learning process; and a visual reference, worked with your own hands, will give you understanding and skill.

A teaching aid in the form of a long, narrow scroll was woven for the workshops I have given and for this book (figures 1-1, 1-2, 1-3). Fifteen different units, as well as long warp ends at top and bottom, show about fifty ideas and techniques. They are "thumbnail" size, but the results are there to study, expand, and adapt. You can weave a similar reference/sampler for use as a reminder and reference. The size or shape is not as important as the learning, but try to make an attractive composition and pay attention to color (this, too, is part of the whole experience). Be sure to make a list or chart of—or label in some way—the different areas as you proceed so you will be able to identify them later. For ready reference, type a companion scroll that gives brief information about each unit and hang it beside the woven scroll (figure 1-1).

1-1. Scroll of techniques and ideas, with typed scroll giving descriptions.

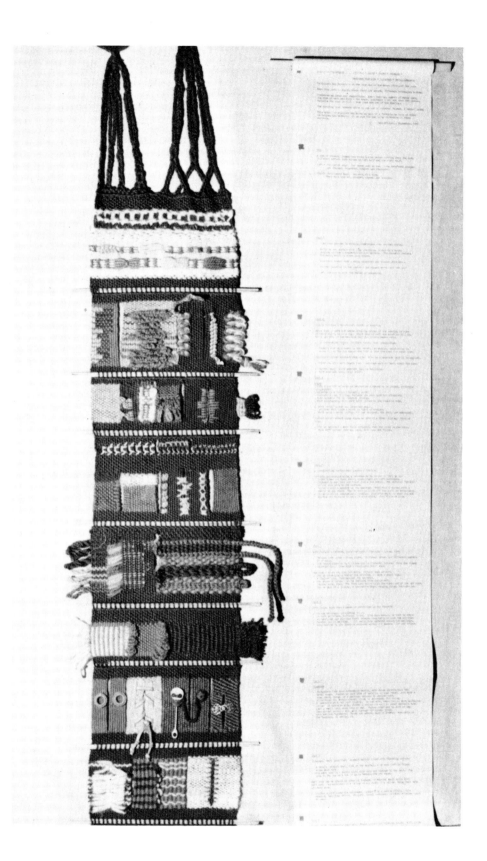

The Woven Scroll

The progression on this scroll follows procedures approximately as taught in my workshops and is presented here for ideas and suggestions, but you will want to make up your own sequence and selection. Exact spacing, number of warps used, the kind of warp and weft—the weave and placement—are all your own choice. The warp and basic weft used here are the same: a fine, strong rug wool. Additional wefts are: pearl cotton, handspun wool, chenille, and tapestry wool. Each was chosen to express a certain method. Colors are limited to the medium brown of the warp and weft, and to lighter brown, natural white, grayed green, and grayed and bright yellow. The reference sampler is about 9" × 90", with almost a yard of extra warp length at each end to allow for warp manipulation such as braiding.

Changes to a different technique in a reference/sampler will be easier to pick out at a glance if there is a dividing line and a change of color. In the reference/sampler shown here, colors were changed with each new example within each unit. The same brown as the warp was used for all of the woven areas between examples; it was also used for some of the techniques in order to give a unified look.

To divide the units, one row of oriental soumak was worked and two bamboo picks woven in. Strips of cardboard or heavy or bright yarn could also be used for dividers (wide strips of cardboard were placed to space the fringe and were left in). The edge technique is worked just above the spacer. Because the woven scroll is rolled and packed and used as a reference, the bamboo picks give it some stability. The typed scroll, slipped into a plastic spine top and bottom, is rolled separately, then rolled up into the woven one. Put in a small plastic bag, the reference/sampler and scroll are ready to travel or file.

Description of Units

Read the scroll from bottom up, the way it was woven, and from left to right where the units have more than one technique across. Figure 1-2 shows the bottom and the first seven units.

Bottom: The warp ends are finished after the weaving is cut from the loom. To more clearly show the groupings of warps, all the grouped ends are caught together in a tie-wrap about six inches down. Next, a short, fat, three-stranded braid is made and then the ends are divided into three bunches, wrapped, and tied (see chapter 2).

Unit 1: To secure the edge and group warps for fringe, first weave one row of Greek soumak, six warps in a group. Weave two more rows of Greek soumak, then several rows over two and under two warps. Continue to weave over one and under one. Note the lacy, open pattern formed by this progression from bundled to single warp ends (see chapter 2).

Unit 2: Warp ends are confined with a wrap-and-split technique (woven version of the Rumanian embroidery stitch), in alternate groups of four and six warps (see chapter 2).

Unit 3: The weft is wrapped around two warps, *very* snugly, three times. This is less reliable than the two methods mentioned above, but is satisfactory on a clinging wool fiber, or if the edge will not be subjected to a great deal of movement and wear.

Unit 4: Four rows of Greek soumak, in a contrasting color, are worked over six warps at a time. Warp ends are then divided into groups of three and a single row of Greek soumak woven. A deep, lacelike edge can be developed by repeating the rows of knots and dividing the warp groups up in different ways. It looks much like the wide macramé borders on Mexican rebozos, but is easily accomplished right on the loom before weaving the rest of the textile (see chapter 2).

Unit 5: This consists of vertical column variations. These are alternatives to plain wrapping, which is not always practical or dependable:

- Five versions of the half-hitch go in one direction (which spirals) over one, two, three, and four warps.
- Three columns of alternating half-hitches of homespun wool have knots all falling along the same side.
- Alternating hitches form a zigzag pattern of spirals.
- Spiral hitches alternate with a few rows of plain weave.
- Chenille, wrapped, forms a pattern of connecting warp groups (see chapter 2). Chenille is an excellent choice for wrapped warps because it is smooth and clinging.
- Plain wrapping is worked, with some columns over-crowded to cause bowing (a careful, even tension results in a straight column).

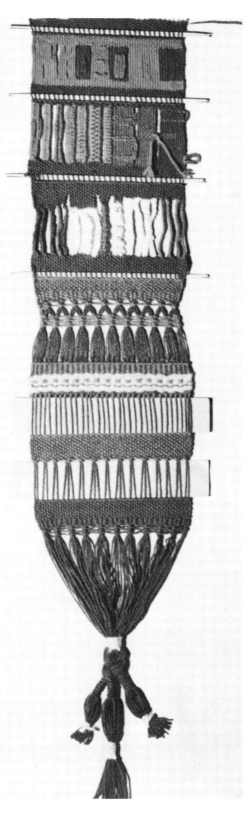

Unit 7
Chapter 5

Unit 6
Chapters 2 and 5

Unit 5
Chapter 2

Unit 4
Chapter 2

Unit 3

Unit 2
Chapter 2

Unit 1
Chapter 2

Bottom
Warp Ends
Chapter 2

1-2. Bottom half of the woven scroll.

Unit 6: Columns in more techniques are shown in the left half of this section:

- Wrap-and-split with slit weave is shown in the center. Buttonhole-stitches over two warps are at each side of the slit.
- Wrap-and-split, straight up.
- The woven figure eight is shaped by pulling weft in then relaxing it, but keeping a very firm and even wrap.
- Four columns, variations of oriental soumak, closed fashion.
- Five variations for buttonhole or lacing loops and ties at edges:
  - One row of chaining is worked close to the selvedge for a flat, large loop.
  - Two rows of chaining over the warp continue out from the selvedge and back to form a loop.
  - Three woven rows with long ends which are braided for a tied joining.
  - A long, narrow loop at the selvedge.
  - A small, round selvedge loop.

Unit 7: Woven slits for various purposes are shown here:

- Two small sections woven with random slit placement.
- A vertical loop is placed anywhere it is needed. One or more warps are lifted and blanket-stitched.
- Two horizontal loops have extra weft added and are buttonholed.
- A wide, woven tab or loop, for belts or hangers, has extra warps added for the width and length needed, then woven.
- Plain weave with long slits represents two edges for joining or for a closure.
- In the narrow section at the far right, one row of oriental soumak is woven to represent a hem turning (this does not show much here, but see more about this in Hems, chapter 2).

Figure 1-3 shows Units 8 through 15 and the top of the scroll.

Unit 8:

- To represent joining or fastening of two pieces, small sections were woven, with a slit between.
- Weft ends are woven and left hanging along the right selvedge on one piece and the left selvedge of the second for a tied joining (the ends lie flat on the surface).
- This is the same weft tie idea, but the double

knot is tied and the ends put back to the other side. The tied join appears to be a row of textured knots, with no fringe (see chapter 3).
- A blanket stitch is worked along facing selvedges, ready to be joined with a needle stitch or crochet. It could be laced, whipped, or overcast. Here, the join is Rumanian stitch (see chapter 3).

Unit 9: Four closure ideas are presented here. Slit-weave sections are woven separately to represent the two edges of a coat, for example. Then the closures are added (see chapters 3 and 5):

- Two rings are covered with a buttonhole stitch. This is the true tailor's buttonhole stitch, with the extra twist for a firm edge for better wear. Rings are sewn on each piece, then joined with a tie, thong, or chained cord (see chapters 3 and 5).
- Slits are woven in, evenly spaced, along the selvedge for lacing. They are laced with a leather thong.
- A pick and cord closing has two horizontal loops on one side and on the opposite side, a button. Knot or chain a cord, with a loop at one end. Fasten the pick to the other end. Slip the loop over the button and slide the pick through the loop.
- Hook-and-eye fasteners. These are pewter, made in Norway.

Unit 10:

- Handspun wool weft loops along the selvedge give a casual, full-fringed edge.
- Weft loops, closely spaced, form a rounded ridge. Smaller and larger loops appear on opposite selvedges.
- A textured tab is made along the selvedge. Weft ends are extended and became the tab warp. Six passes knotted in the Damascus warp-end finish create an edge trim with a texture that echoes the basket weave. The ends are cut. This is a trim, or part of a join.
- The plain-woven sections are left so stitches or trims can be added to the reference/sampler (see chapter 2).

Unit 11:

- This shows twisted weft loops in three sizes, with different yarns and numbers of strands used:
- Cut fringe is laid in. Different colors of weft

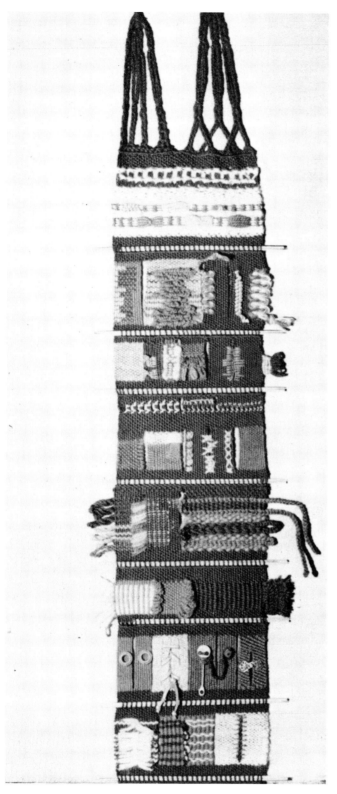

Top Edge
Warp Ends
Chapter 2

Unit 15
Chapter 5

Unit 14
Chapter 2

Unit 13
Chapter 2

Unit 12
Chapter 2

Unit 11
Chapter 2

Unit 10
Chapter 2

Unit 9
Chapters 3 and 5

Unit 8
Chapters 2 and 3

1-3. Top half of woven scroll.

are woven an inch or so into the edge and back out again. An intricate border design can be made in this simple fashion. Ends can be short, long, cut, or loops.
- Several woven-chain tricks are shown here (read from bottom up):
  - Two chained rows and several chained loops.
  - Double weft, chained "bump" at left selvedge, chained loop at the right.
  - Chained weft ends, for ties or trim (see chapter 2).

Unit 12: Strength and texture can be achieved along a selvedge to be joined or left as is:

- One Greek soumak begins and ends each row of weaving for a subtle selvedge interest. Try it with contrasting color, too.
- Oriental soumak, closed fashion, goes back and forth over a few warps, with the vertical accent at the turn adding to the texture.
  - Needle stitches worked as you weave:
  - Sorbello stitch marches up the selvedge.
  - Sorbello stitch adapted as a joining and as an edge stitch, worked in different proportions.
  - A plain weave area to fill with stitch examples.
  - Hemstitch variations: ladder, plain, and trellis.

Unit 13: Edges are shown in this section:

- Venetian lace stitch. Crocheted points on the the selvedge are used for decoration or part of a join. For directions, see *Encyclopedia of Needlework* by Therese de Dillmont (see Bibliography).
- Buttonhole open filling stitch is worked in triangles on selvedges. Points are joined with overcast stitch for an airy join. Weft loops are picked up at selvedges. There are large and small loops.
- Picked-up weft loops are filled in with figure-eight weave. These are shaped to an oval or elongated small tabs. Place them anywhere: along edges, scattered, or in a pattern for surface texture. One, at right, is left unwoven to show the first step.
- Continuous Ghiordes knot loops, close together, suggest a looped fringe. Countered oriental soumak rows above are used for a heading.
- Blanket stitch variation is worked along the edges for part of a later join or trim.
- Selvedge tabs. Weft loops are taken out from the selvedge to become warps for a few rows of Greek soumak. Ends are left in loops (see chapter 2).

Unit 14: Double selvedge (reinforced, Coptic, or Argatch) has short rows of weft woven in when the center of weaving is heavy rows of knots, as in a rug, and rows of ground weave at the selvedges are not close enough:

- Just the double selvedge is shown, woven in contrasting color and no center heavy rows, to indicate where it is needed.
- The center is filled with pile weave, and the double selvedges are added in contrasting color. At the top of the example, the extra wefts have not been put in to show where it is needed.
- Three examples of a Peruvian-inspired woven tape. Two are adapted and woven on as an integral part of the weaving. The narrow one, of pearl 5, is woven as a separate tape to be applied (see chapter 2).

Unit 15: Embellished overshots are done on the loom. The surface is enriched by long overshots, which are woven or knotted to form bow or other shapes. One unit, at right, is unwoven to show the first step. The overshots can surface from a loom-controlled pattern or they can be woven in by hand wherever you wish (see chapter 5).

The top edge and warp-ends: Two rows of Greek soumak are worked over groups of warp with handspun white wool weft. This is followed by about an inch of plain weave, then a row of oriental soumak. When cut from the loom, the warp ends were finished as follows (different methods were worked on the left and the right halves of the warp):

- Left: Philippine edge with two warps used as one. Long warp ends are then grouped and braided in a three-strand braid. They are then separated, braided, and regrouped.
- Right: Philippine edge, one warp at a time. Warp ends are braided, grouped, crossed, and braided.

PHASE II

Phase II concerns learning embroidery stitches for joining or embellishment, edge stitches, and other techniques on already-woven cloth. Workshop students usually go back to their woven reference/sampler and add stitches and trims in the woven areas left for that purpose. This phase is also of use to nonweavers who work

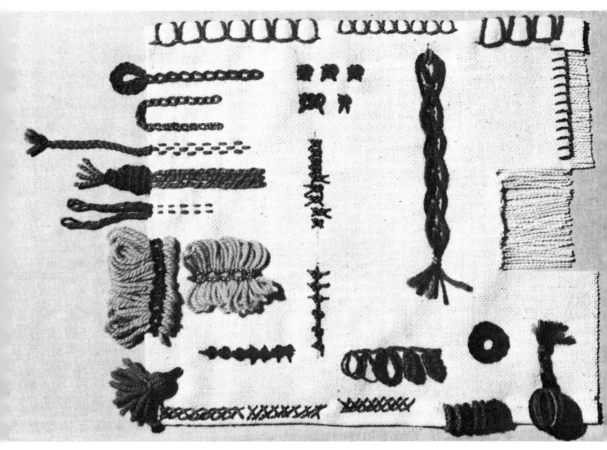

1-4. Reference/sampler of needlework and of applied trims. This sampler shows eighteen finishing techniques.

with purchased textiles. Fashioning trims, tassels, fringes, and closures to be applied is a part of this section. The visual aid for Phase II is a reference/sampler on cloth (Figure 1-4). Another good way to learn embroidery stitches is to work each one on a separate cloth, trying many variations and finding those that will work for joining, edge finishes, and/or surface textures only (figure 1-5).

For Needleworkers

A special message to needleworkers—those who sew, embroider, and stitch: this book is for you, too. Workshops on the subject of fabricating and finishing are taught to embroiderers, as well as to weavers. Many of the techniques and methods detailed to be part of weaving in Phase I can be achieved with a needle and thread on woven cloth. Some, interpreted in needlework, will give

the same effect as when woven. For example, needle chain stitch can be extended into a chained loop for a buttonhole, lacing, tied join, or ornamentation of the edge, as in Unit 6 of the scroll. A needle running stitch is more like a plain weave, with ends taken out beyond an edge and braided for a tie. Oriental soumak is woven, but on cloth the outline or stem stitch gives a similar result. So, look at the woven ideas and see how many can be adapted for needlework.

The Cloth Reference/Sampler

A small reference/sampler for some finishing methods off the loom is shown in figure 1-4. There are countless other techniques and methods; these few, chosen for workshops, are representative of the scope of this subject and can quite easily be sampled in a short time. De-

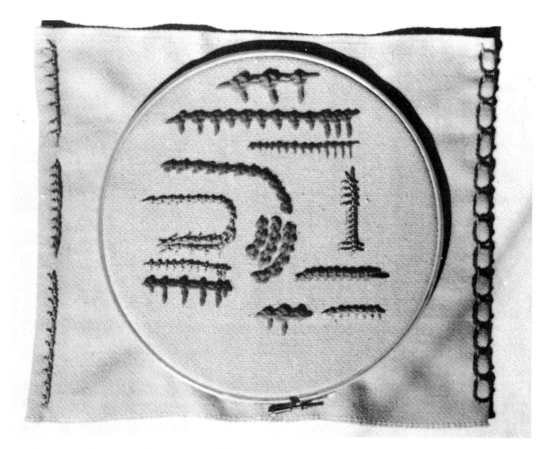

1-5. Exploring stitches on cloth in a hoop. This sampler shows the Palestrina stitch with variations; the Eskimo lacing edge stitch is on the right.

velopment and directions for all of these are detailed in subject chapters.

- Closed herringbone stitch on hems
- Wrapped edge and dangle, from a Bolivian Coca bag
- Mini tassel
- Palestrina stitch as a surface texture and as a joining stitch
- Loops, buttonholed and woven in a figure-eight tab
- Buttonholed ring for part of a closure
- Fastfringe, and two ways to apply it
- Running stitch with twisted fringe beyond the edge
- Three rows of overcast, with edge tab in Greek soumak
- Three alternating rows of running stitch, ends braided for a tie

- Two chain stitch rows, with chained flat loop at the edge
- Chain stitch row, with chained loop at the edge
- Sorbello stitch variations as a surface texture and as a joining stitch
- Five-strand joining
- Cloth cut and threads pulled, to work a bit of Philippine Edge, with two strands, then four strands
- Blanket or buttonhole stitch above fringed edge to hold the weft in place
- Across the top, Eskimo lacing edge, in three sizes

You may wish to do several small cloth reference/samplers, or one or several large ones as you find other ideas to try. Explore stitches in depth, independently, and when a need arises.

EXPLORING EMBROIDERY STITCHES

Figure 1-5 shows one of the teaching aids used for learning and adapting selected embroidery stitches. This is a good way to analyze conventional surface stitches. Try them a number of ways to see if they join, if they cover an edge, or how they are best used as an embellishment.

One other way to show ideas and methods in small scale is on woven bands. Some of the examples in the following chapters are shown this way. A large number of plain weave bands, of wool knitting worsted, with long lengths of warp at each end, were woven for me by Harold Tacker. Then I had the pleasure of trying all kinds of edges and joins and warpend finishes on them. Figure 1-6 shows one.

Four methods of sampling for reference and learning, on and off the loom, are shown to help you devise ways of sorting out and experiencing techniques of interest and use to you. Time is used to maximum advantage when you are trying out and learning!

1-6. Small samplings on a woven band include one row of Philippine edge, then ends braided, with colors separate.

SELVEDGES

Selvedge treatment encompasses a wide range of effects and uses. Selvedges are a basic part of the weaving. Think of them as more than just the margins. For strength, extra selvedge yarns may be added to the warp, doubling or tripling two or more warp threads along the edge. For design, these added warp threads at the selvedge can be in various colors for a striped edge; or they can be of thicker yarns or multiple strands for a ridge; or they can be wide, to make a band of contrast, which can either be threaded in a loom pattern or embellished with needle stitches for a trim. Decorative bands or braids can be woven along the selvedge and are complete trims to be left as is or further embellished with stitches as the weaving progresses. Bands or bindings can be woven separately and applied.

An embroidery stitch chosen carefully to relate to the pattern of the band, matching or contrasting, will widen it and add richness to the trim. Good, straight selvedges are required of individual bands, too. Needle stitches worked along the selvedge as weaving proceeds may be a part of a later join or trim. When selvedges are a part of a conventional sewn seam, there are no raw edges to cover or turn under. Widths and shapes can be woven to size so there are selvedges instead of cut edges. Right and left selvedges may have different treatments of color, pattern, or texture. Crochet, needle stitches, textured yarns, picked-up loops, and patterns all may be a part of the woven selvedge.

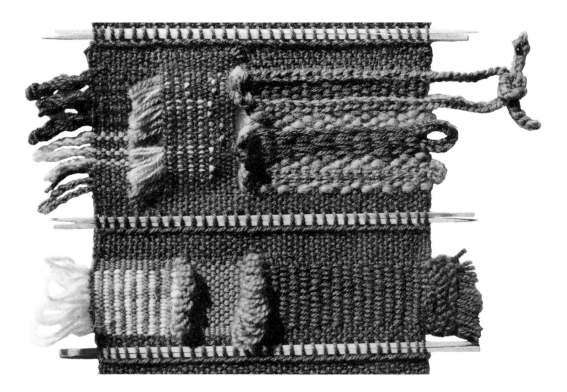

2-2. Units 10 and 11 from the scroll. This shows seven different extended weft ideas.

2. Edges, Ends, and Hems

Edges can be either selvedges or cut edges. Ends are warp ends that may be hemmed or fringed. Beyond these simplistic definitions is an almost unlimited scope of techniques and variations. A selvedge can be much more than a strong, evenly woven right and left edge. A cut edge can be more than a plain hem. A warp end can be more than a plain fringe or a turned-up hem. An edge is half of a join. A join is plain or fancy. A fancy join is a trim. A trim with tassels and fringes and stitches is an embellishment. Some of the methods that will be discussed in this chapter are familiar and often used; but I have also experimented, researched, and explored to find new and different ways and I am sure you will think of more.

Planning and decisions made for end and edge finishes begin with the overall design plan. *Where, how,* and *what* are the key words to consider when you plan your weaving. Where and how will it be used? How will it be woven and finished? What special preparations must be made for further finishing? All of these factors determine the selection of warp, weft, sett, size and color of yarn, and sometimes the choice of loom. Edges, either selvedge or cut, are finished in many different ways. When they are to be joined, the various seaming methods must be considered along with needle stitches that may be desirable. For this reason seams are briefly discussed in this chapter and more fully in the chapter on joining. Decisions on the treatment of ends and hems should also be made before you begin. Ideas and methods follow. Plan for a warp-end finish on or off the loom, for hemming, or for one of the other ways to complete your weaving.

2-1. Edges, ends, hems—and an African pulley and reed loom. (Suede and wool coat by Susan Snover; tapestry coat detail by Eleanor Van de Water; Chinese embroidered purse, courtesy of Beverly Rush)

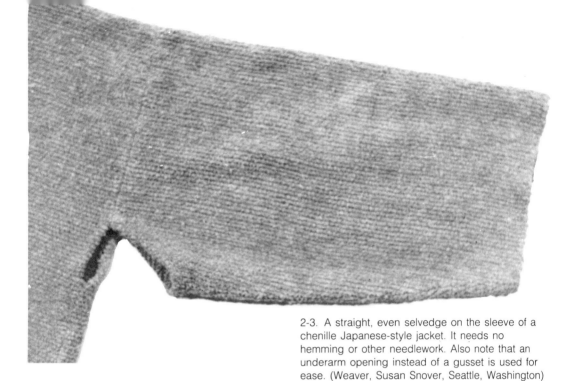

2-3. A straight, even selvedge on the sleeve of a chenille Japanese-style jacket. It needs no hemming or other needlework. Also note that an underarm opening instead of a gusset is used for ease. (Weaver, Susan Snover, Seattle, Washington)

The Practical Part

An even selvedge is a mark of good weaving and pride in craftsmanship. A well-woven edge is especially important when the selvedge is to be visible. The first thing to do about selvedges is to learn to weave them carefully. The second is to select the proper selvedge for your project. Practice and experience will add up to a straight edge with no narrowing and few loops or scallops. A loose warp with uneven tension will not permit a smooth, straight edge; it will pull in and the beat will be uneven. Controlled weft turns at the selvedge and a relaxed weft are necessary; arc or angle the weft as you put it into the shed. If the weft is put in straight or taut, the turns around the selvedges will not be smooth; they will be drawn in, distorting the edge. With practice, you will learn just how wide an arc is needed to avoid loops and looseness in the row and at the edge. Even beating of the properly laid weft also helps to create a consistently straight edge. It is also wise to measure the width once in a while. In the concentration of weaving, a narrowing may not be noticed for a few inches. This happens quickly while weaving plain-weave tapestry; intent on the color changes and firm beating, you may find that the edge is curving in before you know it.

2-4. A curved selvedge as even as this shows experience and skill. This example is at the bottom of a chasuble. (Weaver, Anita Mayer, Anacortes, Washington)

An aid for achieving even width and straight selvedges is putting a guide warp through the reed (not through the heddles). This extra warp is woven in every row or in every few rows. It also serves to strengthen the edge. Another aid, especially useful for weaving rugs or other heavy textiles, is the temple. This is an adjustable bar, reset as the weaving progresses, with teeth at the ends; these hold the edges out to the right width.

Another consideration is the requirement of your woven project. A rug, which must have a firm edge for wearability and good looks—and to stay put on the floor—will need to have several doubled or tripled outside warp threads; a double selvedge might be required (see figure 1-3, Unit 14). Fine weavings, such as table textiles, may need only one doubled outside warp. Let the warp sett, size of yarn, the weave, and the project dictate the exact number of strengthening warps you use or whether they are necessary at all. When weaving yardage, doubled selvedge warps help to keep the edge even. Sometimes a single, but heavier warp is the best choice.

Specific types of weaving also have their own special requirements for selvedge warps. For example, tapestry weave requires a strong selvedge warp, but a lacy, open stole may not need extra edge warps. Yardage that will be cut and sewn usually will not need extra selvedge strength to keep the width even. As with all of weaving, use your best judgment as to what is necessary for your product. Notice that some plain-weave tapestries have a ribbed or ridged selvedge edge. This effect is achieved when some of the selvedge warps are of a larger yarn or when several ends are used as one; this can also be exaggerated to become a part of your design. Strength is added, but you also get a neat ribbed edge—a point of good craftsmanship.

The Aesthetic Part

A plain but beautifully woven selvedge is an integral part of design in weaving. With preplanning, the selvedges can add to the total design as you weave. An excellent example of this is seen in the understated, well-done sleeve detail on the chenille Japanese shopkeeper-style jacket shown in figure 2-3. The evenly woven selvedge at the wrist needed no hemming. Plain machine-stitched seams and a narrow turned-in hem on the underarm opening are appropriate and do not take anything away from the focal point of the jacket—the cardwoven binding sewn all around and the inkle-loom woven sash. Some simple but effective ways to enhance an edge follow. These suggestions will perhaps add another facet of design to your weaving so that you will always consider the possibilities of more than a plain selvedge as you weave.

Look about you for ways to finish edges: you may find one that offers a surprising idea. Look at baskets (figures 2-75 and 2-76). More and more baskets are available and many from other countries have unusual treatments. They relate to stitches and weaving because that is what they are! The shallow basket of flat splints and rough wood strips in figure 2-76, for example, suggests a pattern to weave along an edge, something like the triangles in figure 2-9.

Selvedge Accents

There are many ways to accent the selvedges, both practical and aesthetic. Most strengthen the edges while adding distinction to the design. One of the methods used by weavers of Navaho rugs and saddle blankets employs pairs of extra selvedge warps, often in a contrasting color (figure 2-5). These are twisted or twined in their special way as the weaving progresses, appearing to be an outline stitch. In the figure-eight edge, a matching or different-color yarn in a separate hand bobbin is woven along the selvedge in a figure-eight, like the second column in figure 2-60. Over two or more warps, it gives a raised edge, a braided look, and a neat border. To avoid a slit, this extra weft must be caught into an adjoining warp every row or two. This is done the same way as the double selvedge in figure 2-8. A heavy or doubled weft will create a ridged edge line.

Other techniques suggested for weaving verticals or columns (figure 2-60) can become part of a selvedge also, forming a textured border. A shaped or scalloped edge, using just the regular weft, is formed by increasing and lessening the tension of the weft as it is taken around the warp; the shaping is even, so that it looks planned and not just like careless weaving (refer to the shaped column in figure 2-60).

Weave patterns in plain weave or soumak or

2-5. Navaho saddle blanket with extra selvedge cord of gray wool.

Greek Soumak

The Greek soumak technique (figure 2-6) is three half-hitches on one warp, one above the other. It has the satisfying holding quality for protecting weft at warp ends, grouping warp for fringe, or adding texture and strength at the selvedges. It is ideal for open weaves, solid weaves with knobby surface, pattern, and tabs, to name a few. It seems to be the right choice of technique so often that I use it somewhere on almost every weaving.

To weave Greek soumak, refer to the drawing in figure 2-6. Three half hitches are worked around one warp, one above the other. Follow the arrows. Begin by tying the weft around a warp (or group of warps used as one), with the end facing away from you. This is the first encirclement of the three. Dispose of the end by holding it close to

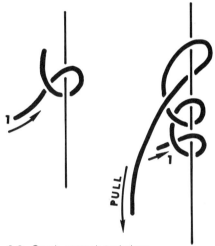

2-6. Greek soumak technique.

2-7. Three Greek soumaks on pairs of warp at a rug selvedge. The white rows are worked in coarse yarn to show the effect.

tapestry techniques, like the triangles in figures 2-9 and C-11. A line of warp color, as shown in a classic example of accent at the selvedge of a Sherpa coat (visible in the detail) in figure 2-40, is achieved when two warps of a contrasting color are entered at each selvedge an inch or two from the edge of the 12" width. When the coat is put together, the simple lines of color make double lines of trim at the side seams and where the sleeve is sewn on. This idea can be expanded by the addition of several different warp colors. An edge trim can also be patterned by threading a loom pattern the width required, or by utilizing one or more of the several weaver-controlled techniques such as plain-weave tapestry, one of the soumak techniques, or an open or lacy weave such as leno or small slits. The use of colors, laid-in areas, or stripes presents infinite possibilities.

the warp, catching it into the next two hitches. The end can be cut close to the knot. (The end of the last knot can be run down into the knots with a needle. The beginning end can be needled in, if you prefer.) Encircle the warp two more times. As you do this, pull down each time. The knots will settle into place. The special holding quality is achieved by pulling the second encirclement very tightly around the warp. The third one should be a little more relaxed so that the knob is visible; this provides the distinctive texture of this technique. Proceed to the next warp, make three encirclements, and so on.

Work from either direction, but be sure that the weft position is changed when the direction is reversed. (This method is the same as for oriental soumak, closed fashion, as seen in figure 2-61, where the weft always goes around the warp and comes up *under* the over-weft.) The working end of the weft is always facing the direction you are weaving. If the position is not changed, the effect will not be correct, with the knot on top. Remember that, from left to right, the encircling weft is to your left and the working end is to your right. From right to left, the encircling end is to your right, the working end is to your left.

These directions are confusing to read, but if you follow them step by step, refer to the drawing, and remember to change positions each time you change directions, you will find, with practice, that it becomes automatic and easy.

A strong edge, with the bonus of some texture, is woven by working Greek soumak knots over one or several warps at the selvedges, at the beginning and end of each row. The procedure is to knot, weave across, and knot at the other end. With a small shuttle, the knots can be made with the main weft. Another method is to have a separate hand bobbin at each selvedge for the soumak, catching in one warp of the center weaving to avoid a slit. Heavy yarn may cause some distortion of the rows of weaving, but the rows can be beaten in firmly. To correct unevenness, an extra row of weft can be woven across and/or the soumak knots put in every other row. In a fine weave, the knots will be very small and the beat even across the width. Sample this idea with different yarns and setts and see how it works. When Greek soumak is woven on edges to be joined, with a butted seam, an interesting textured band is made and can effectively disguise a slip-stitch join. It can be enhanced by a decorative joining stitch such as Rumanian.

Selvedges on Rugs

There are special problems involved in weaving rugs. They have to withstand rough wear and must be woven so that they lie flat on the floor. A weak spot in rugs is the edge and selvedges must be strong, so special care must be taken. Several methods other than the usual double or triple selvedge warps follow.

I have not seen Greek soumak at the selvedges on rugs, but when working with this technique, a natural development is the use of this strong knot on two or more selvedge warps (figure 2-7). It not only provides an extremely stable and strong edge, but also looks smartly finished and fills in well, right up to a heavier weave in the center.

The double selvedge (figure 2-8) with extra rows of weft laid in is one way to fortify vulnerable edges. A double or filled-in selvedge is necessary when the center sections of weaving are a heavy pile weave (or other technique), causing the ground weave to be too loosely beaten at the selvedges. An extra weft fills in for the spaced weft (figure 1-3, unit 14). This extra weft is wound on a small hand bobbin and is used by weaving short extra rows back and forth at each edge as needed. When the same ground weft yarn is used, the added rows will not be noticeable; but if you wish, since they are a necessity, you

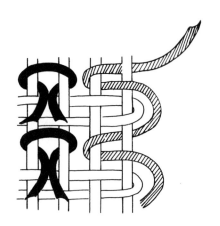

2-8. Weaving the double selvedge.

might make a design element of them, with contrasting color as an edge border design. If the center pile weave is just a few warps in from the edge, the extra weft will probably be covered where cut or looped ends fall over the edge.

Variations of columns are also of use on rug selvedges. All these added techniques stay in place and will not slip apart as a plain-weave selvedge is apt to do with the abrasive wear that rugs receive.

Woven-on Bands

Weaving a decorative band or border at the same time as you weave the body of a garment or household weaving is a satisfying and not too difficult effort. It does take more time on the loom, but when you cut the weaving off the loom you have a handsomely finished edge. Directions are given for just two bands; others, however, can be woven, with variations, from these two methods. Remember that you are weaving two separate pieces of cloth and that they have to be joined by a weft at certain points along the way. Pinpoint slits may be acceptable in some versions, but, essentially, the result is a continuous width with integral border.

An old Mexican Quechquemitl (shawl) provided an idea for a woven-on border. A narrow tape, about ½" wide, of alternating red and white triangles was sewn to the edge of the shawl. It was woven on five warps, the white triangles in an open-knotted technique, the red in plain weave. This suggested another use for Greek soumak and adaptation of the tape to a woven-on edge. Two examples were woven. One, is shown in C-11. The brown wool represents the main body of the weaving in basket weave; the red triangles are plain weave; the green triangles are Greek soumak. The technique is plain-weave tapestry, creating the triangles by weaving on a slant. The dovetail join—turning the main color and pattern color around a common warp, one above the other—is the method of joining the pattern and main weaving. Note that the peak of each soumak triangle stops one warp before the outside warp, so the plain-weave color is continuous along the selvedge.

Another version of the triangle edge is shown in figure 2-9. The method of weaving is similar to the one used in C-11, described above. Two different surface effects are created with the

2-9. A variation of the woven edge shown in C-11. Triangles with texture are woven in Greek soumak.

Greek soumak woven in different directions. At the bottom, the Greek soumak rows are worked on a slant, following the slope of the triangle. At the top, the soumak is worked row by row, increasing then decreasing. In each, the plain weave is attached by the soumak weft catching in one warp of the plain weave. The weaving is done row by row, to the selvedges and back. The plain-weave triangles are woven in rows to the shape of the triangles. Note that even, firm selvedges result because the triangles stop one warp from the edge. The connection between the band and the body of the weaving could be made with other tapestry color-change techniques instead of the dovetail method, which makes a zigzag line. The interlock joining, where the wefts loop around each other then return in the next shed, makes a smooth line. If small slits are acceptable, the wefts can connect only every three or four rows. These various techniques, each with a different look, are part of your design.

Peruvian Undulating Edge Tape

This decorative edge is made on just two warps with four wefts (figure 2-10). In the early Nazca period, it was woven as a separate edge tape, usually very fine and narrow, to be sewn on. My adaptation, woven on as an integral part of the edge, has worked quite successfully. Using four colors expresses the undulating pattern and is also of help in the weaving because it is essential

2-10. Peruvian undulating edge, examples from the scroll. Three versions are shown here: two in wool are woven on to the body of the weaving; the third, a narrow one of pearl 5, is not attached.

to keep the wefts in sequence. The two edge warps (these can be doubled or tripled for strength) are put through the reed, not the heddles, so the opening of the shed to weave the body of the textile will not distort or loosen the edge pattern. The effect is best if all the yarns are about the same size. Knitting worsted, rug yarn, or pearl 3 or 5 are good choices, but fine or unevenly spun yarns do not show the yarn path, which is the distinctive feature of this edge.

To weave the edge as a separate tape, use four weft strands, each a different color, in lengths as long as convenient (although ends of added lengths can be hidden). Leave several inches of weft at the beginning, loosely knotted together. They can later be finished with a tassel, or braided or darned into the weaving. Begin weaving over the two warps, plain weave, over and under. Use the wefts in color sequence—1, 2, 3, 4, then 4, 3, 2, 1—like playing the musical scales. Continue until the edge or separate tape is the length needed. The tension should be somewhat relaxed, but not loose enough to let the wefts loop up. Gently pinch and ease down in place before continuing with the next group of four.

In making a woven-on edge, turn the weft of the main part of the weaving around just the inside one of the two edge warps to close the slit. Weave the row, catch around the edge warp, return the main weft, then weave the four pattern wefts; then go back and forth with the main weft, the four pattern wefts, and so on. If the slit is too open, bring the main weft around after two pattern wefts. Try the system that works best for your yarn and sett.

If a length of the edging is to be woven then sewn on, the procedure is the same. Put two

2-11. Weaving the Peruvian undulating edge.

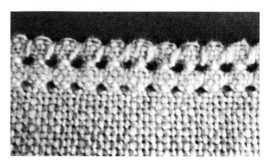

2-12. Detail of a precisely worked edge at the neckline of a linen tunic, with two rows of four-sided stitch. (Weaver, Penelope B. Drooker, Sanbornville, New Hampshire; photograph by Penelope B. Drooker)

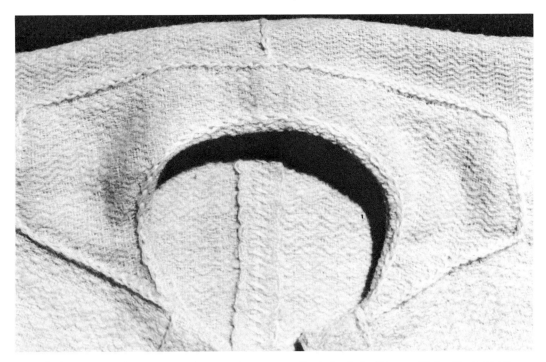

2-13. Facing on a wool coat, cut to shape, and sewn on with chain stitch. (Weaver, Melba Short, Mukilteo, Washington)

warps on a loom, and weave the four wefts in sequence. After you have mastered the basics, try wider bands with three or four warps for quite a different effect; or try more than four colors; or subtly blended shades of one color. Chenille makes a luxurious, rich trim.

The beauty of this edge is in the even, smooth tension, with the turns flat and just touching. It is helpful to practice this on a frame loom in order to learn the correct tension and to sample colors and yarns. The choice of colors and their sequence makes a great deal of difference in the effect.

Facings

Facings play an important part in the construction of well-made tailored garments and can be of the same cut and material sewn on (figure 2-13), of a woven lighter weight, or of a conventional thin material like lining fabric, depending on where and how they are used.

A facing or extension can be woven on at the shoulder, at a side slit, at the neckline, or whenever needed, then turned back and sewn down

by hand, by using the template method. Woven-on facings eliminate the bulk of a seam where an extra piece would have to be added.

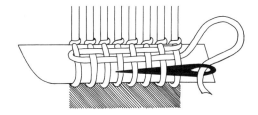

2-14. Extensions woven on for facings. The template is made of lucite, so the warp and weaving show through. The template warp is wrapped around the loom warp.

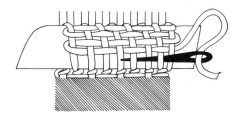

2-15. Weave up and over the template to shape the extension.

Jan Burhen devised a method to add facings at the neckline and side slits of a heavy wool tunic (figures 2-14 and 2-15). She had templates made of thick, strong lucite, so the placement is accurate. Tapered at the end, the template slips out easily. The facing warp is fastened to the loom warp by alternately encircling a loom warp (soumak fashion), wrapping around the template, encircling the next loom warp, going around the template again, and so on, for the width needed. The ends are woven in. The soumak covers the warps and makes a neat edge when the facing is folded down and sewn. Weave up and over the template. Use a long, blunt needle as a shuttle, and firmly beat the weaving on the template. Slip the gauge out and weave ends in. Fold the facing back and sew by hand.

Weaving extensions for facings is a fine solution to an often difficult problem with bulky hand-wovens, and they can be woven right on the loom as part of the cloth. Cutting and sewing on a facing in heavy wool is almost impossible to do without an awkward ridge at the seam; sometimes you may not want to use a different material, so this woven-extension idea is a welcome one.

There are other ways of neatly finishing edges without an added facing. Have a turned-back facing with no seam by weaving extra inches just where needed—for example, on the front edge of a jacket. Weave extra width from the bottom edge to the neck, then weave on a slant or curve to conform to the neckline shape. When assembling, fold back the extended width and sew with a topstitch or a blind stitch. This same procedure works for a turned-back cuff. If the cloth is pliable and soft, a lapel or shawl collar can be rolled back with no seaming or extra weaving necessary (figure 2-33).

Wefts at the Selvedge

Wefts can perform much more than the expected covering of warps and turns at the selvedges. Any number of ways can be found to utilize them for trims, for part of a tied join, or for adding some textural interest along the edges.

Figure 2-2 shows a number of ways that wefts extended beyond the selvedge can form a fringe: for a twisted weft fringe, the weft is carried out and around the skeleton warp for a gauge, then twisted around itself before returning to complete the row of weaving; weft ends can be cut, with a few wefts laid in and back out; a woven chain, with chaining beyond the edge for ties, loops, or a textured edge, can be effective (unit 11); loops at the edge of handspun wool that curls and twists can be used; loops can be picked up at each edge at various heights; and wefts extended to become warps and covered with rows of Greek soumak form a tab that could be part of a join or closure, or just a trim (unit 10).

A "skeleton" warp, an extra warp for a gauge, can be tied to the front and back beams, but not through the reed or heddle. It is merely a gauge placed to regulate the length of the fringe and is removed after the weaving is finished. When released, the loops of the fringe may twist a bit. When a definite twist is desired, the weft is taken out and around the extra warp and wrapped several times around itself before returning to complete the row of weaving.

Laid-in wefts, doubled and in several colors, are shown in figure 2-16. The weft of the main weaving is brought to the selvedge in each row. Each fringe weft is laid in the shed with the ground weave and returned in the next row. Cut each fringe weft twice as long as needed for the weaving-in and the return. For a smooth selvedge line, the fringe and ground wefts are

2-16. Multicolored wefts are laid in for a weft fringe (from the scroll, unit 11).

2-17. Laid-in weft fringe on a band that is sewn around the bottom of a Philippine Igorot skirt. (Photograph by William Eng)

always returned in the same sequence. This idea came from a Philippine skirt (figure 2-17). Short lengths of fine weft were woven in and out, leaving short lengths beyond the selvedge. A pattern could be worked out with wefts of different colors and lengths, or with the weft lifted into a loop where it returns. The band on the skirt was woven separately, then sewn on at the hemline, and is a good idea for adding length to a skirt.

When the weft is extended beyond the selvedge, one precaution must be taken. The extended wefts leave the outside warps floating. Alternating picks of ground weave must return around the selvedge warp to confine the selvedge. Be consistent in the sequence of returning the weft around the edge. Always take it over or under the extended wefts for an even line. This is most necessary when a contrasting color is used and the path of the yarn is conspicuous.

When weft ends are thick and impossible to conceal by weaving back in or to weave as a continuous weft, the obvious solution is to let them be a part of your planned design as cut ends. Strips of rags, leather, fur, huge yarns, or crisp, natural material such as reeds will add some texture to the selvedge edges. Plan and weave them with care, however, so the result is not too rag-tag. The easy trick of weaving a textured edge and taking care of thick weft ends such as leather is illustrated in figure 2-18. The problem is solved by weaving in separate strips.

2-18. Double-faced textile of wool and strips of soft deerskin glove leather. The edges are full, casual, blunt fringes of leather. It is reversible, and the corner is turned back to show the wool face.

The ground weft is carefully woven with consistent turns so the edge will be secure and neat looking. It may be desirable to wrap the ground weft around each cut end before returning it in the shed. If the bulky weft strips are flexible enough, an easy loop can be made at the selvedge and the weft continued for two or three rows.

Applied Edge Finishes

Woven bands, whether woven on an inkle loom, or cards, or on a regular loom, are handsome and versatile for trimming or emphasizing an edge (figure 2-19). On clothing, woven bands can be used effectively as over-the-edge binding, or they can be sewn flat along seams and edges. Woven bands applied to edges or seams add richness—but please don't plan to use them as Band-Aids! You can contrive a cover-up for a poorly woven selvedge, but do strive for a well-woven edge that can stand alone. When bands are applied as a trim, be very sure that the shrinkage factor has been considered and planned for. When an applied band shrinks more than the material it is sewn on does, disastrous puckering will result. So be sure that each part of the weaving has been shrunk before putting it all together. Be careful, too, when sewing on bands to make them nice and flat.

Selvedges or cut edges may also be bound with bias strips; with a binding needlestitch such as closed buttonhole; or with a stitch that covers both the face and reverse side, or they can be hemmed or faced.

2-19. A black and white band is sewn around the neckline and down each edge of the front of a handwoven white wool cape from Finland. The cut ends cross at the back for a small accent. A pewter clasp closes the front. (Courtesy, Anita Mayer)

Bands at the Edges

The chair in figure 2-20 is a good example of how bands can be added. Bands woven in a different but complementary pattern are effectively used to edge the swing-chair. They also add needed strength to the edge. The long length of yardage is fastened around the strong metal-rod hanger by tying the warp ends in several knots; this adds a fluff of fringe along the top. A sofa-sized foam cushion covers a heavy plywood base. The cushion is trimmed with a woven band of knotted fringe that is sewn on at front and back, completing this practical and good-looking woven swing. The warp is black carpet warp; the weft is nylon variegated yarn in red and black. Here is an excellent example of using several finishing ideas in a decorative way.

2-20. Woven bands for a trim and for strength are sewn to the edges of this triangular swing-chair. (Weaver, Jean Kimmel, Somerset, Pennsylvania; photograph by Bowen Studios, Somerset, Pennsylvania)

Knitted Cords as Bindings

Knitted cord can be used to cover a raw edge as a binding (figure 2-21). As you knit the tube (see instructions on page 103), don't draw it up completely at the back—leave it somewhat open.

2-22. Pillow seams are closed and bordered at the same time by sewing on a fat knitted cord with buttonhole stitch. Cord is of heavy wool rug yarn, four stitches on size 10½ double-end needles.

Then it rolls over the edge like a folded tape, is sewn through once, catching on both sides, or sewn on each side. Use an embroidery stitch, slip stitch, or overcast in matching or contrasting yarns. The knitted cord as a binding presents a vast array of possible sizes, colors, yarns, and methods of application. It is a change from commercial bindings and is custom-made for the product.

Knitted cords can also be placed over a seam. A large-size knitted cord in heavy, even-spun rug wool borders a wool pillow shown in figure 2-22. One row of buttonhole stitching in a light orange wool sews the seams together, sews the cord over the seams, and provides a line of contrast, all in one pass. The meeting of the two ends was somewhat awkward and bulky, so the yarn was continued out in a length of crochet chain stitch, turned back, and sewn into loops at one corner for small ornamentation—also for a hanging or carrying loop.

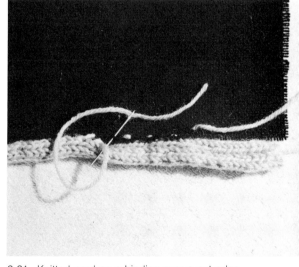

2-21. Knitted cord as a binding over a cut edge.

Binding Cut Edges with Stitches

Learning edge-binding stitches is very rewarding. Whenever an edge needs extra strength for wear, or on a loosely woven textile, or if it is to be reversible, where each face should be attractive—or just for the joy of trying a different method that adds that extra touch—there are stitches to be discovered and learned (figures 2-23, 2-24, and 3-26). Decorative stitches bind the edge of the Chinese silk purse shown in figure 2-25.

2-25. Detail of an elegant little Chinese silk purse. The edges are bound with stitches. Intricate and closely sewn, it looks at first glance like a sewn-on woven binding. It is composed of closely set stitches over the edge. The white pattern is woven into the blue threads. The same technique was worked on the edges of the flap, but with a different pattern. (From the collection of Beverly Rush)

2-23. Reversible Welsh tapestry weave coat with a hand-stitched edge binding on both faces. Blanket stitch is overstitched with several rows of chain stitch (figure 2-24). The same binding stitches are used to join the side seams and the extra strip added around the bottom for length. (By Eleanor Van de Water; photograph by Eleanor Van de Water)

2-24. Combined blanket (buttonhole) and chain stitch.

Basket Edge Stitch

The basket edge stitch is an over-the-edge stitch traditionally worked around needle-made or woven rugs or canvas needlework as a finishing edge, not as a part of the weaving. It firms an edge and helps make it longer wearing; it can be reworked or repaired when worn; and it can cover a selvedge that is not quite straight and true.

Work from left to right (figure 2-26). Hide the knot in the hem, or take two tiny backstitches where they will be hidden by the stitch. Come up at a, then over the edge to the right and up at b. Go back over the edge to the left, up at c, to the right of and close to a. Cross over the edge to the right and up at d, just to the right of b. Go over the edge to the left at e, coming up between c and b. Continue, crossing to the right and then to the left. For a very close covering stitch, keep c only a thread or two to the right of a, and e close to c–b.

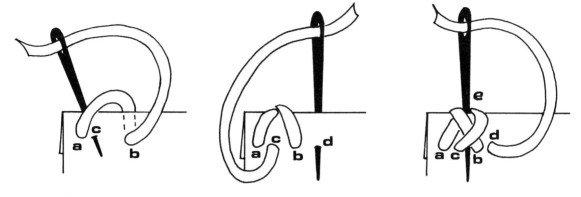

2-26. Basket edge stitch. This covers both sides of the edge like a binding and is also used for a firm joining stitch.

Eskimo Lacing Edge

This edge finish is perfect where you need a reversible edge that looks the same on each side of the cloth. It comes from the edge stitch used by Eskimo women on seal parkas; I found it first in Jacqueline Enthoven's book, *Creative Stitches of Embroidery*. This stitch has become a real favorite, and many uses for it have been found. It works well around a neckline, over a bottom hem, as in the stitchery sampler tunic (figure 3-17), on placemats, blankets, afghans— or back to its origin—on a parka! Use it where both sides will show, as on a shawl, a room divider, or reversible mats.

To work the stitch, pin or baste a turned-back hem, or work on the selvedge. The stitch consists of two passes (figures 2-27 and 2-28): the first pass is a row of running stitches that will hold the hem in place and the second is lacing these stitches. There are several important points to note before beginning the stitches. First, place each running stitch separately, stabbing through the cloth rather than gathering several stitches at once; this keeps the tension on each stitch even, so that the lacing will easily slip through. Second, keep the stitches evenly spaced for best effect. Third, hide the beginning knots of both threads inside the hem; at the end, take two backstitches inside the hem to fasten the thread. Fourth, use a blunt-ended tapestry needle, which does not go through the cloth, for the lacing.

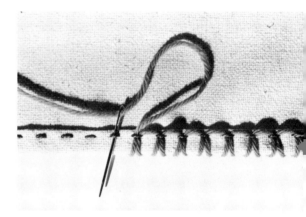

2-27. Eskimo lacing stitch, back view showing turned hem.

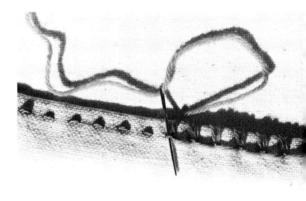

2-28. Eskimo over-the-edge lacing stitch, front side.

The first running stitch *must* be on the top side. The second running stitch, on the back, is where the lacing begins. Otherwise the lacing will not work correctly. Work from left to right, or right to left. Lace from back to front, flopping the hem over and back. The lacing thread does not penetrate the cloth. From left to right, start lacing *up* toward the hem edge, *down* through the first stitch on the front (to your left). Then go to the right, *under* the next stitch, and *up* over the edge. Go *down* through the first stitch (left), *up* through the next stitch, flop the hem, *down* through the second stitch, and so on. Notice that, except for the first running stitch on the top side, each stitch has two lacing stitches through it. Remember that the stitch is a reversible edge finish so it should be neat on both sides.

There are many variations possible with this stitch. Some yarns will make the pattern look like O's, some like V's, depending upon the spacing and length of the running stitch, the depth of the hem, and the height of the stitch. On a large scale, add a French knot or small cross stitch in the circles for more richness. Experiment with uneven stitches for a different effect. Note the edge on the white wool tabard, shown in figure 5-14, which was laced with uneven handspun; the running stitches were placed so the lacing formed rounds the size of the small silver circles holding the side ties. On the edge of a baby coverlet, I used the lacing stitch to sew two layers of quilted nylon together, with pearl 5 for small, delicate stitches. For a solid, braidlike edge covering on both sides of the hem, try this variation; the two sides have an interesting and a different look. For the base stitch, make a row of short outline stitches. The reverse of this stitch has straight, touching stitches like a backstitch. When laced in the Eskimo fashion, the outline stitch on the top side adds an extra row of stitches and looks like a full braid. The reverse side looks much like the one with the running-stitch base, but is close and covering. This little change in the effect provides some unexpected interest. Take care that the underside stitches just touch and are straight and even.

2-29. A pocket for a long vest could also be used as a small bag. The over-the-edge wrapped stitch and pom-pom ideas are from a Bolivian coca bag (C-9). Also see figure 4-43, and how to make pom-poms in chapter 4.

2-30. Over-the-edge wrapped stitch.

Over-the-Edge Wrapped Stitch

An edge finish and pom-poms seen on the Bolivian coca bag shown in C-9 richly fill a hem; carefully done, it is handsome on both sides. Studying the many little coca bags in collections and exhibits—and owning one—I have found several different methods of edge and trim finishes. The one that intrigued me the most is the wrapped edge shown in figure 2-29. Having no idea of just how these were worked, experiment brought forth the following way (figure 2-30).

Sample a wrapped loop before you begin a whole edge to measure the length of yarn needed for one wrapping; adding yarn and hiding ends are awkward on a short wrapping. Also, finish the first stitch before placing the next basic stitch so the spacing will be close enough. There are two passes in this stitch: the basic stitch and then the wrapping of it. Turn a hem and baste or hem it; the wrapped edge will completely cover it. Begin at the back, with a knot hidden in the hem. Make one stitch over the edge and back up to the beginning, just above the hemline. Wrap the stitch and continue until the edge is filled. Start the next stitch close beside the first one, for complete coverage, and wrap with the same stitch yarn or change colors.

To wrap, start at the top of the first stitch on

the back, putting the knot inside of the hem. Use a blunt-end tapestry needle, since the wrapping does not go into the cloth. Wrap the stitch, round and round, placing each row just touching the others. Keep the tension as even as possible. When the stitch is wrapped down the back and up the front, stitch through the cloth to the back. If you are changing color for the next one, finish off the first with a stitch or two inside of the hem. The wrapping of the basic stitches is done the same way as on the pom-pom (figure 4-43).

An easy position for wrapping is to place the hem over your finger, between thumb and first finger, as when hemming. Then the thumb can help control the tension as you wrap down and around and back up the stitch. The wrapping yarn may start to unspin or twist from the wrapping motion. Just let the end hang loose and let it spin into shape again. Roll the wrapped loop gently between thumb and finger to even out. The larger the wrapped stitch, the heavier and firmer the textile should be, both for easier working and for no sagging from the weight of the stitch. This edge stitch is perfect for a join of two layers of cloth, as used along the bottom of the bag in figure 2-29 because the two layers are firm and accept the weight of the yarn.

Yarns and Variations for Wrapped Stitches

Smooth-spun wool such as knitting worsted or crewel yarn make even wraps. Some wools are so springy and crisp they will not stay wrapped. Pearl cotton and cotton floss wrap smoothly for small-scale work. Chenille is ideal, especially for a rich, thick rolled edge. Make the basic stitch with cotton or wool yarn, then wrap with chenille. A stitch an inch long on each side is about minimum for the bulk of the chenille; even longer is better and more in scale. The wrapping yarn can be continued from one stitch to the next when just one color and yarn is used. You can also vary the look with buttonhole stitches instead of wrapping over each stitch. One or more rows of stitches can be worked above the line of wrapped loops to define and enlarge the edge finish, but it is complete and looks finished "as is." Over-crowded wrapping causes the loop to twist and spiral, so unless you want that effect, try to make the wrap evenly spaced. Making the pom-pom dangles in the same stitch is explained in chapter 4.

Ways to Use Crochet

Crocheted edges and inserts, wide or narrow, are observed on many handwoven garments and other weavings. Crochet is a wise choice of technique. It looks good, is quite easy to do, and complements the texture and construction of handwoven textiles. It can be quite solid and firm or loose and elastic to suit the need. In figure 2-31, wide bands of crochet edge the panels around the bottom of the Shan Coat by Anita Mayer. The coat also has crocheted inserts at the shoulder, and all edges are finished in narrow crochet. Note the uses for crochet as a joining in chapter 3, and for crochet buttons and loops in chapter 5.

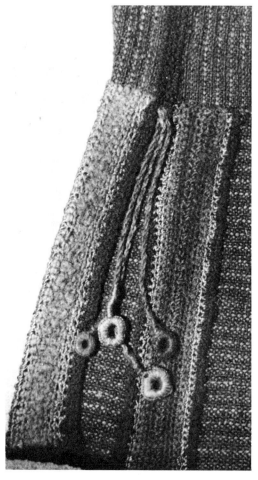

2-31. Wide crochet edges the loose panels at the bottom of the Shan coat. (By Anita Mayer, Anacortes, Washington)

2-32. Knitted cuff on a woven wool coat. (By Susan Snover)

Knitting and Handwoven Textiles

Knitting is another natural blend of techniques with handwovens. For collars, cuffs, waistbands, and edges, weavers often combine knitting and weaving. Just one example is shown here (figure 2-32). A very satisfactory way to draw a sleeve in at the wrist is to knit a cuff. When it is of the same or similar yarn and color, it looks right and appears more slimming than a full straight sleeve, particularly in heavy wool.

Machine-stitched Edges

Usually, I suggest covering a necessary machine-stitch with a hand-stitch to present a completely handcrafted product. But machine-stitching has decorative uses, too. A completely simple and direct edge and seam finish is seen in figures 2-33 and 2-34. On a purchased sleeveless jacket of lightweight wool flannel, every edge and seam is machine-stitched in matching thread closely covering the unturned cut edge. A shawl collar rolls back softly. There is no seam there. Pockets are stitched on with no turn-ins. The side, shoulder, and collar seams just barely overlap. This not only presents a beautiful "canvas" for possible future hand-stitched embellishment, but is elegant and uncluttered for now. This concept is a natural for flat edges and seams, especially for heavy

handwovens. A rolled-back shawl collar like this could be widened and shaped in the weaving as an extension, as mentioned in the section on woven-on facings.

2-33. Machine-stitched edges on a flannel jacket. The shawl collar is simply rolled back; it has no seam.

Surrounding Edges

Edges that surround a weaving seem important to mention. Often a conventional wooden frame or just a top-hanging rod are not the best solution for a woven wall piece or tapestry. A woven border, or a surround of woven cloth or stitches, is complementary to a small tapestry.

Background for a Small Weaving

How to mount a small tapestry or other weaving is sometimes a difficult decision. My own preference follows the traditional mode of hanging large tapestries unframed. Small tapestries seem to need some kind of background, even when a border is woven on as part of the design.

2-34. Pocket and edges on the flannel jacket are machine-stitched, with no turned-in hem.

A suitable background is provided by using harmonizing cloth—preferably handwoven—stretched and stapled to a canvas-covered artist's frame (C-7). To mount the Nativity tapestry shown in figure 2-35, row after even row of close buttonhole stitches in the same deep blue wool used for the woven sky were sewn on linen rug canvas. The center, where the tapestry was sewn, was left uncovered. Then the whole piece was wrapped over a piece of plywood and laced securely on the back. The tapestry can be hung, stand on a mantel or table, and stay smooth in storage between holidays. The thickness of the weaving creates a shadow-line and gives depth.

Another way of acquiring an integral surrounding edge for a weaving on a frame is to use either an attractive picture frame (reinforce the corners) or a stretcher frame, wound with yarn or painted, as the loom. The warp holders are short nails along the top and bottom, at the back. The weaving is framed by the loom.

2-35. Surrounding edges. A border for a tapestry is made of rows of buttonhole stitches on rug canvas. Yarn is the same grayed-blue of the sky in the tapestry.

WARP ENDS

The warp ends at the top and bottom of a weaving require some kind of treatment so the body of the weaving will not ravel. Choice of method should be well thought out before warping the loom is begun in order to provide for ample length. There are several other considerations to keep in mind. Warp ends can be left exposed in a straight or grouped fringe; knotted or braided; long or short; tasseled; or with no fringe and ends darned in or hemmed. Also, there is a choice of several warp-end techniques that can be used to secure the weft, for example, the Philippine edge (figure 2-50).

The natural choice for a warp-end finish is a fringe. In the section on fringes, you will find examples of more elaborate warp-end finishes that go beyond the serviceable weft-protector methods in this chapter.

Selection of Warp-end Finishes

There is a warp-end finish for just about any need. The following are a few of the possibilities. Ends to be finished off the loom can be darned

2-36. Darned-in ends disappear.

in to give a smooth edge with no apparent cut ends (figure 2-36). Wrapped and woven ends can shape a rounded corner at each selvedge, or just on one side, or scallops can be made along the end (figures 2-46 and 2-49). A braided look is created by Czech (figure 2-42), Indian (figure 2-45) and Philippine (figure 2-50) edges. A knotted edge is shaped by the number of rows worked and whether it is worked always from the same edge or back and forth, or from the top or bottom, or alternating (figure 2-47). A hem that rolls back up on the edge results when several rows of Damascus edge are worked from the same edge each row (figure 2-52).

Ends can also be finished on the loom. A row of Greek soumak bundles warps for the fringe (figure 2-38). An open pattern from the sequence of soumak rows is another possibility (see unit 4 of the scroll). Whenever possible, accomplish as much of a warp-end finish on the loom as feasible.

Instead of cutting the whole textile from the loom in one swoop, take a bit more time to secure the weft with whichever technique you choose—the Indian edge, for instance (figure 2-45). Cut just two or three ends at one time, work the technique, cut a few more, and so on. Securing the weft is infinitely easier to do while the textile is in place, so restrain your eagerness to see the weaving off the loom. Of course, further finishes can be done later.

Greek Soumak at Warp Ends

A small wall weaving of firmly spun wool (figure 2-37), all in white—without the distraction of color—illustrates some of the versatility of Greek soumak. Here, the point is the secure and smooth line along the warp ends. At the top, after removal from the loom, the warp ends are taken over an aluminum rod and then to the back. With a needle, a row of the soumak is worked on the right side over groups of warps to hold the ends in place at the back; this also adds a textured line at the front. Long warp ends at the back are wrapped into a collected edge (figure 2-43). Half of the warps are collected from left to center; the other half, from right to center. The bundle of ends is trimmed and shaped. Both sides are presentable. (The weave on the back side will be quite different, showing the vertical wrapped warp effect, which is the soumak in reverse.) The top end

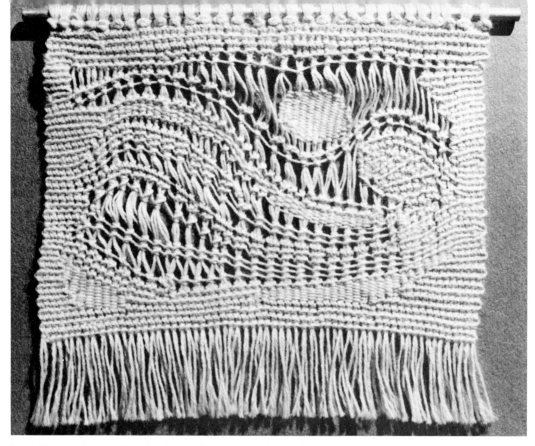

2-37. Small white wool hanging in Greek soumak technique. Top and bottom are secured with the soumak edges, woven on the loom.

could have been stopped with the final row of soumak, with straight ends cut like the bottom edge, and the small hanging mounted on a frame covered with cloth of a dark or bright color to give depth to the open weave. Mounted on a rod and hung out from the wall, the play of shadows adds another dimension.

Warp-end Groups—Plus

An extension of the idea in unit 4 of the scroll, grouping the warp ends for fringe with Greek soumak, is shown in figure 2-38. Above the divided groups, an open weave appears as the weft expands into a regular weave. Triangles of weft are formed. That suggested the idea of weaving within the triangles for a firm edge and a chance for a patterned border. The example in figure 2-38 began with groups of sixteen warps; the weft was then woven over eight, four, and finally, continuing the plain weave, over two warps. These open wefts became warps, turned sideways and woven; at the left of the photograph

you can see these wefts woven up the triangle, then down, leaving long ends. Weave as many rows as are needed to fill the space. Knot the ends and cut them even for a small tassel between the triangles. At the right plain weave fills the space, woven up and down (held sideways), with the ends tucked in at the back. These two

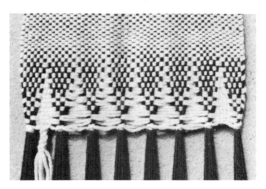

2-38. Greek soumak at bottom edge groups warps for fringe. Long empty wefts become warps. Weave in the triangular spaces. Add a weft-end tassel. Try these ideas along a hem.

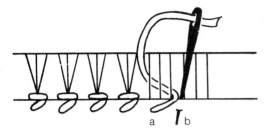

2-39. Simple hemstitching. It draws several warp threads together in a tight little stitch. This drawing of simple hemstitching shows three warps enclosed. Come up at *a*, in the cloth, just below the first warp of the group. Then go to the right and back of the warp group. Draw up and, from back, come out at *b*, ready to work the next stitch.

2-40. Hemstitching variation at the hem of a Sherpa coat. (Weaver, Lois Anderson, Seattle, Washington)

2-41. This sample weaving of a loom pattern is now a pocket. The warp ends at the top and bottom were hemstitched on the loom. It was folded over for a pocket flap, and stitches were added to continue the woven pattern into the hem.

finishes are woven in matching yarn, but a contrast would give a colorful pattern. If you want both ends of the weaving to be the same, this triangle effect can be woven at the other end of the warp, in reverse. Count the rows of weft and the number of warps per row in the groups, gradually spreading the warps apart until the last row, which is the soumak grouping. The weaving in the triangles is done last, before cutting from the loom.

Pay close attention to the tension of the weft. Unless you want the weft to be loopy and loose between the woven warps, pull it straight, but not tight and pulled in. Ease the weft in and down to the previous row. Spread the warp groups by gently tugging at each side, both at the same time. When removed from the loom, the width may draw in some and the wefts over the open spaces may be somewhat loose. These effects are adjustable in the weaving for the effect you want to achieve. Refer to the scroll examples for other versions of warp-end weft guards.

Other Warp-end Techniques, On the Loom

Hemstitching on the loom is a tried and true edge finish. In figure 2-40, a variation of hemstitching protects the weft and provides a neat edge with short fringe at the hem end of a Sherpa coat. Note the accent of darker gray warp along the selvedges. The drawing in figure 2-39 shows how to do simple hemstitching.

Small reference/samplers are useful. A sampling of pattern weave hemstitched at each warp end is shown in figure 2-41. The size of the piece suggested a pocket, with the top folded over showing the color of the pattern in reverse colors. It is black and gold fine mercerized cotton. The black plain weave at the end is woven on the sample to illustrate the idea of a fine weave to turn back and sew for a hem. It is much thinner and will give a flat end finish. A subtle embellishment on the pocket flap is a row of embroidery stitches extending the woven pattern. Straight and Y stitches repeat the shapes and are sewn with the same gold color in the weave. This is another bonus idea from a small sample—a new pocket on a black skirt!

Other Warp-end Techniques, Off the Loom

Select the method of securing warp ends to fit the circumstance. On a textile already cut from

2-42. Czech edge warp-end finish. The braidlike finish is orderly and neat. Follow the numbers, and notice the progression here of each warp end first going *under* the next one. The result is a straight fringe. Also see figure 4-9.

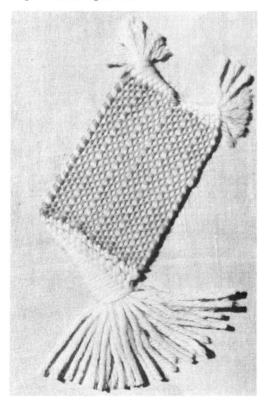

2-43. Examples of the collected edge on the ends of a sampling band.

the loom, with warp ends loose, one of the methods like the Philippine edge is somewhat easier to do neatly than the wrap and weave, for example. When you knot any of the warp-end finishes, pay close attention to just where the ends are placed—and why just there. Note that after each encirclement and dropping of an end, the next move holds the end in place. It is a series of overs and unders in the sequence of the particular method. Several examples follow.

In the *Czech edge*, the first warp end (figure 2-42) goes under the next one, then back over, then under. So, logically, the end that is on top has to come down and is held there by the sequence of over and under. Analyzing and really seeing where the yarn has to go in any weaver-controlled technique helps you to learn and remember the sequence. As you sample and try techniques, a better method may become apparent: perhaps an easier way to accomplish a tie, or dispose of a loose end, or the best time to perform a certain step in sequence.

The warp-end treatment for a *collected edge* (figure 2-43) is just what it says. The ends are collected, each warp in turn, hitching around all of the warps (figure 2-44). Start from one selvedge, ending at the other edge with a triangular bundle and a fluff of ends. Or begin in the middle and work both ways; shape the cut ends. Or begin a new group every inch or so, for a sawtooth edge. Plan to have extra long warp ends

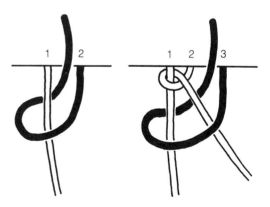

2-44. Collected edge. This is called accumulated edge in macramé. Each warp end is collected in succession by the next one. Carry all of the ends along, pulling each hitch up snugly to the edge of the weaving. The ever-increasing bundle will result in a wedge-shaped edge with the last few ends in a burst of fringe.

so you can have an edge with elaborate tassels. This finish is very conservative with fine warp ends, or bold with large yarns.

The *Indian edge* is one finish that shapes warp ends; it is alternately worked from opposite ends, turning the weaving over and working from the back, then on the top side again (figure 2-45). Leave long, long warp ends at the end of the weaving to experiment with. It's fun and surprising to see what you can do with this technique. Examples an are shown in figures 2-46 and 2-47.

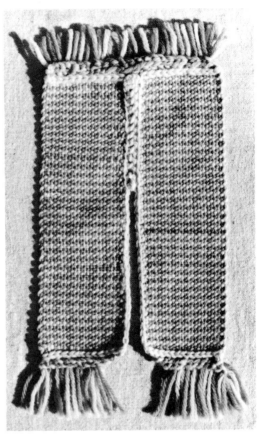

2-46. Warp ends shaped by a sequence of rows of Indian edge. This example is on a sampling for a vest.

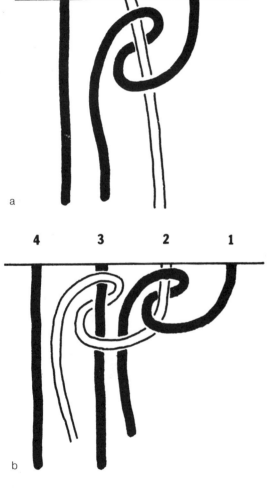

2-45. Indian edge. This neat edge is worked from right to left in the drawing, but can be worked from either direction. The warp ends first go *over* the next one, then under and over and hang down. Work close to the edge of the weaving.

Figure 2-46 shows a miniature version of a vest or stole made from two rectangles. The front corners are rounded by rows of Indian edge. The back edge is straight with a short fringe. To assemble and finish, single crochet is worked along the two inside edges (the selvedges are left plain); the crochet edges are laced back and forth for a join at the back. To shape the front sections, on the left, work two rows of Indian edge, right to left, then turn it over and do one row left to right; on the right section, work two rows left to right, turn, and do one row right to left. (Turning to the opposite face and alternating directions causes the rounded corner. The shape is controlled by the number of rows in one direction before alternating.) For warp ends at the back, work the Indian edge across the warp ends of the joined sections, on the top face only, starting left to right then back, right to left; warp ends can be cut very short for a straight fringe, or they can be darned in. One row of needle chainstitch above the Indian edge is a final touch, like a continuation of the crochet edge. The sides could be closed with a knotted cord tie.

Warp as Weft

A shaped-end finish or a whole triangular weaving can be woven almost magically when warp becomes weft. Figure 2-48 is a small example woven off the loom with the cut warp ends at the end of a band. When done this way, it is a matter of weaving, in turn, each cut warp end over and under the remaining ends (similar to warp ends wrapped and woven). The warp ends here are used double, woven in a basket weave. The last three pairs of ends are wrapped and tasseled. For a variation, weave in small sections like this all across a width, starting at the center and going both ways, much like the suggestions for the collected edge.

The same process can be followed as a final finish *on the loom*. For an entire triangular weaving, warp a frame or other loom. Calculate the length of warp needed for the size of the project. The weaving proceeds by cutting warp one, weaving it into the remaining warps; cutting and weaving warp two; and so on. The diagonal side is the selvedge, and the other two sides will need some edge finish to secure the fringes. Try it for a shawl. It consumes itself!

2-47. An exaggerated example of warp ends shaped by Indian edge worked from each side and on the top and bottom faces of the weaving. Ends are finished with collected edge.

2-48. Warp as weft. Points can be woven with warp ends when each warp becomes weft.

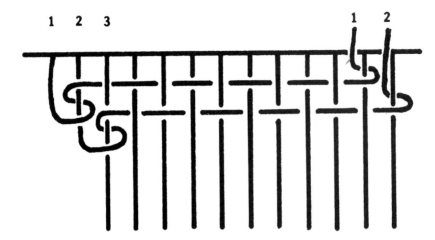

1 2 3   1 2

2-49. Wrapped and woven warp-end fringe finish—a simple but secure way to protect the weft. Each warp, in turn, is wrapped around the next warp then woven over and under until used. The end is pulled up, and the rows are beaten up close. When all is woven, the ends can be cut short or darned in.

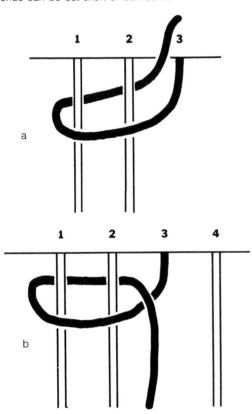

a

1   2   3

1   2   3   4

b

2-50. Philippine edge. This warp-end finish is shown worked from left to right, but it can be reversed. The wrapping end (3) is taken over two ends at once. Number 1 is dropped and number 4 wraps over warp ends 2 and 3, and so on. The result is a straight fringe, and a definite braided look at the edge of the weaving.

Warp Ends Wrapped and Woven

This method is much like the warp as weft in figure 2-48. It is much easier to do this as the weaving is being cut from the loom; cut one warp at a time and weave in. Off the loom, weight the cloth then wrap and weave the ends from the back. It is easier to place the ends and they can be darned in if desirable. Keep the over-under sequence of the last row of weaving for a smooth transition into the protector technique. The ends are pulled up at the back and can be trimmed short after all is completed. Work either from right to left, or left to right, all across. Use warps in pairs or singles. For a different look, work from the center out in both directions.

The *Philippine edge* makes a plaited-looking edge with a straight flat fringe. One row is secure, but several rows make a decorative band. It is much like the other wrapped end finishes, but has a distinctive look because two ends are wrapped at once rather than single ends. The handbag of fine wool in brown and white loom pattern, shown in figure 2-51, has a Philippine edge. At the ends, just the stripes in the pattern are woven in the hem, which is turned to the outside over a dowel. The warp-end fringe was more than twice this long, so one row of Philippine edge was knotted for a strong line, then the ends were cut to show more of the square and diamond pattern. A wide crocheted band joins each side. The bentwood handle, made by the weaver, is stained brown and looks just right. A lining of cream sateen finishes the inside.

2-51. A thoughtfully designed handbag with the hem and woven-in stripes folded to the outside and sewn over a dowel. The warp ends are secured by a Philippine edge then cut into a short fringe. (Designer/weaver, Helen Gray, Leesburg, Virginia)

The *half Damascus* and the *Damascus* are weft-guarding edges. The half Damascus (figure 2-53, *a*) is a perfectly satisfactory edge in itself. The warp ends lie up on the fabric and can be darned in, cut short, or covered with a band. Consider this and work from the back face when you do an edge this way and want the ends on the back. When several rows are worked from the same edge each time, an attractive plaitlike hem is made. The Damascus edge (figure 2-53, *b*) continues the same method as above, but you will bring the warp ends back down so they hang in a straight fringe. In both, a ridge is formed along the edge; in half Damascus, it is on the back, and in Damascus it is on the top. Play with these, singly or alternating the two, and you will find some very interesting effects are possible, from a knotted ridge to a wide band.

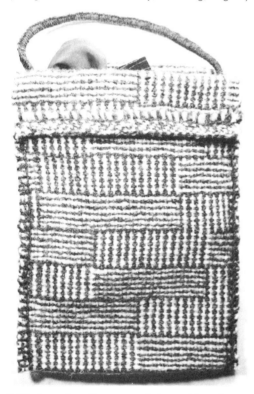

2-52. A wool muffler, woven in log cabin pattern, was folded and sewn for a double-pocket handbag. Different weft protector techniques were worked on the two flaps. Shown here are three rows of half Damascus edge with a very short fringe, rolled up as a hem and sewn with a row of backstitch; and buttonhole stitch over cotton roving cord for the handle.

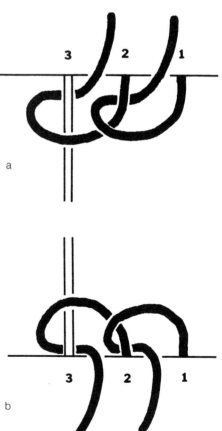

2-53. Half Damascus (*a*) and Damascus (*b*) weft-guarding warp-end finishes. With half Damascus, the ends face up on the edge. Damascus, the second pass, brings them down in a fringe.

2-54. A saddle blanket (detail) with twined warp-end finish and a pair of plaited cords with tassels, but not fringe. (Spinner/weaver, Carol Bodily, Redmond, Washington; photograph by Harold Tacker)

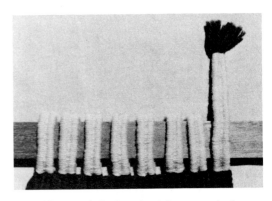

The saddle blanket of handspun wools in natural colors (figure 2-54) has *twined warp ends*. The twining yarn is continued out at the corner then knotted into cords with tasseled ends. The warp ends are twined, in succession, and pushed up close to the fabric edge (figure 2-55). This is a simple, straight edge with no fringe. For a smooth result, allow several inches of warp-end length.

Tabs and Columns

Tabs and columns are similar in construction. Both are woven over just a few warps, in any number of different techniques. Tabs are woven either for an edge or end finish, like a woven fringe, or folded back to make loops for hanging or other uses. Columns are woven within the weaving for vertical accents, open weave, or as borders.

Tabs

Weave *tabs* for a hanging loop warp-end finish. In figure 2-56 the tabs serve as hangers with a wood strip slipped through. One tab is shown unsewn. The width and length of the tabs are determined by the product. Measure the circumference of the hanging rod to be sure the length of weaving is adequate for a wall weaving or drapery. These tabs are quite stiff and thick, sized to accommodate the wooden hanger bar. Warp and weft is wool knitting worsted. Eight warps are grouped and woven in the wrap-and-

2-56. Warp ends for hanging tabs woven in the wrap-and-split technique (woven Rumanian stitch). One is left unsewn, as it would be for tab fringe, to show length and fringed end, which is sewn at the back.

2-55. Twined warp ends. A ridged edge that holds well is formed. No ends are left hanging. Follow the numbers, weaving warp number *1* under warp *2*, over warp *3*; warp *2* under warp *3*; and so on.

split method, shown in figure 2-57, the woven version of the Rumanian embroidery stitch. About an inch of warp ends is unwoven. The tabs are folded over to the back and sewn to the woven edge. A fringe of ends also makes a nice decorative touch if the weaving is to be hung where both sides are visible; the tabs can be folded over to the front side and a feature made of the fringed ends sewn on with a showy needle stitch.

The straight tab at the right in figure 2-56 shows how a tab fringe is done. The same methods for bottom fringe and hanger tabs make a unified frame for a wall piece. The tabs, woven straight and firm, have short, cut warp ends at the bottom to soften and to avoid a blunt stop. It is also a more practical way to end the tabs, as it would be difficult to weave this many warps back in. This is another example of "designing in" any ends that are impossible or awkward to dispose of.

To weave *warp tabs* on the loom (figure 2-58), warps are divided into groups of four and woven in plain weave, with about two inches of

warp left for tying on the tassels. The tabs lie flat, but the tassels are full so they spread and flare. To knot tabs off the loom (figure 2-59) at the end of a woven band, three rows of Czech edge (figure 2-42) are worked over single warp ends. Then two warp ends are knotted in overhand knots across the width for a narrow row of openwork, then three more rows of the Czech edge are worked. Warps are divided into four groups, each one knotted into an individual tab by about eight passes, back and forth, of the Czech edge. The tassels are tied on with the warp ends in a double knot, which is hidden inside of the tassel. The simple tassels are made and attached easily. Measure and cut a bundle of yarn twice the length of the finished tassel.

2-58. Flat plain-weave tabs with tassels tied on with the unwoven warp ends.

2-57. My woven version of the Rumanian embroidery stitch, named the wrap-and-split technique (because that is the structure), is shown as a column or border, but it could also be woven as a band to be applied. Compare it with the embroidery stitch (figure 3-30) and note that the only difference is that in weaving, the catch-down in the center comes up from below. The sequence is: bring weft up from back of warp *1*, over both warps, around and under warp *2*, up over between warps and to the left, under warp *1*, ready to come up and begin the next pass. Use a needle or hand hank as a shuttle or bobbin.

2-59. Tabs knotted off the loom, tassels tied on.

Lay the yarns out flat and even, over warp ends. Tie with a double knot. Fold yarns over and wrap a strand of yarn around a few times, tie, and a tassel is formed.

Weft tabs are also a possibility. They have both practical and decorative uses. A small example of a woven weft tab is shown in figure 2-2. The wefts are extended out from the selvedge, become the warps, are woven, and a tab is made along a selvedge. A weft tab could be used for decoration, as part of a closure, or as a button or snap tab. If slits are woven in the tab, it can button to the opposite side.

Try to make all tabs even in width and along the edges. Ease and squeeze with thumb and finger as you wrap or knot each weft. Keep the tension even so warp coverage is not loopy and loose. Test the length you need before weaving a whole row of tabs and find the take-up of the hanging rod. For example, a finished tab, two inches long, sewn at the back, with a one-half inch rod slipped through requires a woven length of six inches; a flat one-inch-wide rod will require a tab that is woven about five inches long. The hanger should slip through easily.

If a drape is to be opened and closed then gathered into folds, the tabs must be long enough for ease and should be sewn firmly. Another factor to consider: if a very heavy yarn is used and the tabs are stiff and thick, as in figure 2-56, added length will be needed to accomplish a smooth roll-over plus sewing. To sew the tabs into loops, on narrow tabs with just a few warp ends, darn the ends in, then clip. Darn ends into a few rows of weft and bring to the surface for short fringe below the tab rows. Tab loops can be used as an alternative to skirt bands. On handwovens bands sometimes create a problem with bulk or awkward gathers. Tab loops, woven as an extension at the top edge of a skirt, are a solution. Wide, flat tabs, folded and sewn into loops then belted, are smoother and less bulky. Narrow loops when belted will slightly gather the skirt top. Measure the width of the belt or tie and allow for thickness to assure that the belt can easily slip in and out. Woven tabs withstand wear better than wrapped warps. Even tight wrapping tends to loosen with wear. Finally, if a tab hanger is an afterthought and not a part of the weaving, the tabs can be cut, folded, and sewn on. Narrow woven bands can be sewn on for tabs—an even better idea, because the selvedges don't require a turn-in.

Columns

Columns are alternatives to plain wrapping for vertical units. Wrapping doesn't stay neat in some situations and is sometimes not too successful. Also, most columns will wear better, while adding interest with knots and textures to your design. Expansion of these ideas is only limited by your own interpretation. Weave them over two warps or ten—your choice depends on what you want or what is needed. Refer to figure 2-60 for a variety of techniques. In alternating half-hitches (1), the knots all fall to one side. The figure eight (2) is plain woven back and forth, shaping in and out by regulating the tension of the weft; wraps should just touch, not overlap. For plain-weave columns with small slits (3), two bobbins are necessary for weaving the slits—one for each side; then one is cut, the end tucked in, and weaving is continued with one bobbin. For half-hitches all in one direction (4), spirals, the half-hitches are interrupted by a few rows of plain weave, which creates the flat oval. These half-hitches could also be made to spiral in one direction (5). Numbers 6, 7, and 8 in the illustration are variations of oriental soumak, closed fashion (figure 2-61); note the vertical accent that occurs at the turn in this type of oriental soumak when the position is reversed to weave in the opposite direction. A woven version of the Rumanian embroidery stitch is wrap-and-split (9), so called because the term is descriptive of the method used (figure 2-57). The final example (10) is another spiraling half-hitch.

Ends are sometimes difficult when columns are being wrapped, hitched, or woven. Often a way has to be invented to fit the specific place, but here are a few ways. Hold the beginning end parallel to the warps (to be caught in by the first several encirclements) about a half inch or more; extra length can be snipped off when the work is finished. If the columns are inset, surrounded by weaving, the ends can be woven

2-60. A variety of columns in several techniques: (1) alternating half-hitches; (2) figure eight; (3) plain weave with small slits; (4) half-hitches all in one direction, spiraling, alternate with ovals of plain weave; (5) continuous spiral of half-hitches all in one direction; (6, 7, and 8) variation of oriental soumak; (9) woven version of Rumanian embroidery stitch (wrap-and-split); and (10) another spiral of half-hitches all in one direction.

in. The half-hitch is a secure way of beginning or ending a column. Crown the column with several hitches. The ends of any column can be threaded in a needle and run down in.

Yarn Length for Wrapping

Estimating the length of yarn for wrapping, surface textures, pile weaves, and so forth is chancy. The best method I know of is to work a small example in the exact sett and yarn, then take it apart to measure how much yarn was used; or, measure the yarn first and keep track of the length. This is important if you plan a large project and must have adequate yarn to complete it. Also, it is usually difficult to start a new piece of yarn in the middle of these techniques. If you do have to add a length, it can be done in the same manner as starting, with the end parallel to the warp. Place the new end and the old at different spots along the warp to avoid a thick lump.

HEMS

Since this book cannot be a thorough how-to-sew treatise, only those methods that are suitable for handwovens or are part of the weaving are detailed. Others are mentioned by name for you to look for in any one of the excellent books and magazines on sewing and needlework that are available in bookstores and libraries.

Hemming methods accommodate the fabric and use. There are numerous choices. Sometimes an unorthodox solution is right, and a treatment on a handwoven textile may not be a truly proper tailoring procedure. For example, hemming a heavy handwoven wool with a turn-in will result in an awkward ridge and too thick a hem; use a needle stitch over the cut edge for a flat look. Cut edges and warp ends, especially on a loose weave that easily ravels, should be inconspicuously machine-stitched first, plain or zigzag, then covered with hand-stitching or a seam binding. In figures 2-33 and 2-34, the edge of a close, fine flannel has finished edges

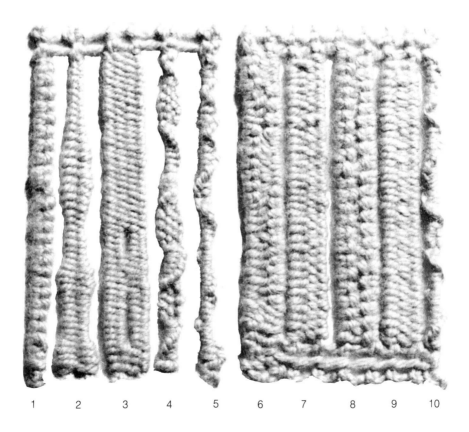

| 1 | 2 | 3 | 4 | 5 | 6 | 7 | 8 | 9 | 10 |

of matching zigzag. When a selvedge is at a hemline and is even and firm, the hem can be blind-stitched or sewn with a decorative topstitch without a turn-in.

There are often some surprises when even the most carefully planned weaving is ready for finishing. The fabric may be more elastic, a bit heavier, or too crisp to flatten in a hem, so you should be prepared with some remedies. There is usually some way to overcome the problem, and often the solution is better than the planned method. The worn old cliche "necessity is the mother of invention" is very nearly dogma in the world of weaving. Following are some solutions for particular kinds of needs: for heavy weave, for one that ravels, and for inconspicuous or showy finishes, among others. Some are familiar ones, and some you may not have seen before. Take a fresh look at edges and ends. Specific examples follow.

Hems on the Loom

Will a turned-up hem be the finish? If so, weave an inch or more with a finer weft for the turn-up (figure 2-41). Use a weft yarn in the same color but of a smaller size; use one ply if the weaving is in a larger yarn. If suitable, a matching cotton or linen can be used on wool. Precaution: the cotton should be preshrunk so there will be no puckering in the hem after shrinking.

A finer, thinner inch or more of hem is often seen on coarse-linen table mats. They lie neatly flat on the table. Consider this, also, for wall pieces that need flat hems. Plans to weave the finer extension for a hem will require careful measurement as the weaving progresses so that

the hems will come at the right place—especially on table mats. If this is impractical, perhaps one of the following methods for a flat hem would be preferable.

For a crisp edge on a turn-back hem, working one row of oriental soumak, closed fashion (figure 2-61), where the hem will be turned helps to make a flatter crisp hem edge, especially in a heavy fabric. Sometimes a thick weave will just roll back and is hard to flatten, even with pressing. While turning, the soumak row can be moved so it is just at the back, or right on the edge. It can be woven in the same weft yarn, in a finer spin of the same color, or in a subtle color accent. This edge row can also be done when the hem is woven in a finer yarn in order to lessen the bulk when turned and sewn. It is helpful, too, to mark the place of the hem as an aid when a long length of placemats or runners is woven. I use it also on tapestry when a hem is the bottom and top finish.

Flat Hems off the Loom

All of the following can be used on any weight material, but are especially suited to heavy ones. For a flat hem on heavy material, eliminate the turn-in with a finish off the loom. Stitches that completely cover the edge and keep the weft from ravelling allow the hem to be turned up just once (figure 2-63). Zigzag or plain machine-stitching right at the edge is a safeguard, especially on a loose weave; then the decorative stitch can be used for the hemming.

Double rows of even running stitches, very close to the bottom edge turn, flattens the hem and adds a neat finish. This was seen on the hem of a very old Asian robe of plain-weave fine cotton. The garment was almost completely covered with embroidery, and this hem finish continued the surface stitching right to the very bottom edge. These ideas tame a balky edge and ornament it, too.

Another way to flatten a hem or edges in heavy materials is to handpick the edges, which is taking tiny running stitches close to the edge. Sew them in one at a time, evenly spaced. The hem edge on the heavy linen skirt in figure 3-21 is finished in this way. This final touch is seen on finely tailored wools and gives an elegant, professional touch of handwork, especially on handwovens that don't press to a really flat edge.

2-61. Oriental soumak, closed fashion, over four warps and back two. Follow the arrows.

The Adaptable Herringbone Stitch

This stitch proves useful in so many ways that every weaver should master it. For hems, it adapts from wide, fine-thread loose stitches as tailors and dressmakers employ it (figure 5-20) to purely decorative applications. When worked with stitches close together, it is called closed (or close) herringbone stitch. The slanting stitches, placed close together, completely hide and protect a raw edge with a solid line of stitches. This truly adaptable stitch can be a firm, attractive joining stitch with stitches close or, for a looser join, with stitches further apart. See figure 3-36 for directions on how to work the closed herringbone as a joining.

It is also called "shadow stitch" when worked on sheer cotton where the stitch shows through on both sides. In this use, the slanting stitches are usually on the under-side, the backstitch on the top side.

If you like the look of two rows of stitches on the back, both rows can be taken through the cloth. For a single row of backstitches on the back, just the bottom row of stitches goes through the cloth to the other side. The top row of stitches is put through just to the inside of the fold.

Refer to the section on joinings and compare this stitch with basket stitch, figure 3-37, which looks much the same, but has a vertical stitch on the back.

A critical point of hand finishing on a hand-woven garment is the hem. Too often an otherwise beautifully finished skirt will have a lumpy hem. To avoid this, use the closed herringbone stitch, which covers the cut edge and eliminates the need for the extra turn-in that causes the unsightly ridge. Machine-stitch the edges first to prevent ravelling. These stitches will be covered. For instructions on how to work this stitch, see figure 2-62.

Linen Vest Project

A vest is an ideal garment for exploration of shapes, hems, embroidery stitches, and other embellishments. Figures 2-63 through 2-66 show the results on a heavy handloomed linen from Belgium. The techniques and methods I wanted to try out were:

- cutting two fronts and the back, first refining the shape and the fit with a muslin (figures 2-64 and 2-65);
- completely finishing each of the three sections—hemming and embroidery—separately, then joining shoulders and sides with a Rumanian stitch as the last step;
- using the herringbone stitch for a flat hem with no turn-in;
- using the "bonus stitch" idea of working a stitch on the top-side, using the rows of backstitch, the back of the herringbone hem, and the Pekinese stitch;
- embellishing with rows and rows of other

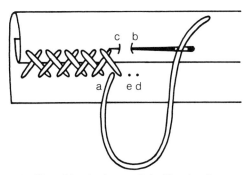

2-62. Closed herringbone stitch. The drawing shows the stitch worked from left to right on a hem folded to the inside. Place the stitches further up on the hem or where it seems best for your use. Keep stitches as even as possible. Come up at a; then a slanting stitch is taken to the right and through the cloth at b. In the same motion, put the needle through to c. A slanting stitch is taken down, to the right, to d, then a horizontal stitch left to e, which begins the next cross. Also see (6) in Figure 3-36.

2-63. Closed herringbone hem on a linen vest, worked on the inside. The hem is turned just once. The two rows of backstitch on the top side become the base for two rows of Pekinese stitch.

stitches and a large motif on the back and each side of the front; and achieving the richness desired by using pearl 3 in the same muted grayed blue-green of the linen.

The results were as successful as I had envisioned them, but the color was all so subtle that it was difficult to photograph well! A skirt was made of the same linen, with hand-picked hem and lapped back seam sewn with buttonhole stitch (figure 3-21).

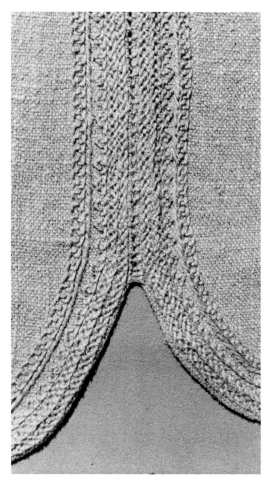

2-66. Side detail of linen vest, showing the Rumanian stitch joining; the two rows of Pekinese stitch close to the outside. Buttonhole, Y, and outline stitches are some of the others used.

2-64. Front view of linen vest, showing the shape and the rows of embroidery. Note that the large motif on each side is half of the single large embroidery on the back.

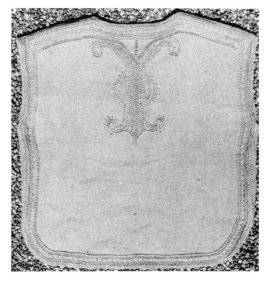

2-65. Back of linen vest.

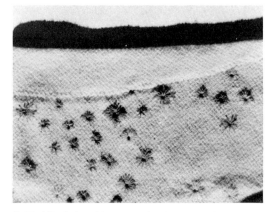

2-67. Wool shawl hemmed in closed herringbone stitch, which covers the cut edge.

Pekinese Stitch as a "Bonus"

This decorative stitch was used as part of the linen vest project. Instructions for working it are in figure 2-68.

This stitch, which is composed of a row of backstitches that are threaded in little loops, adds richness to borders. The two rows along the edge of the vest shown in figure 2-66 are very effective. It can be worked in curves to outline a motif, or in even rows.

Using both sides of an embroidery stitch, when a stitch on the top side makes the base for another stitch on the reverse side, requires some careful placing and checking of each stitch so that it comes out on the reverse side exactly where it needs to be. This made for slower work with the herringbone stitch on the vest, but leaping along with the Pekinese stitch on the top side was a breeze! The second pass, threading through the backstitch, does not pick up any of the cloth. This worked so well, working pairs of stitches for a reversible textile has become another source of study and trials.

Openwork Hems, On Loom and Off

A row or more of hemstitching or leno put in just above and before weaving the rows necessary for a hem is a special designer touch. If it is an afterthought, the same effect can be done on already-woven cloth by pulling a few threads and working with a needle. See figure 2-69 for a drawn-thread border on a linen tunic. Also see two other uses of hemstitching at the very edge, with warp ends in a fringe, in figures 2-40 and 2-41. Hemstitching at the bottom hem, wrists, and round the edges of a jacket gives an elegant and distinguished finish.

Household textiles also benefit from special touches. Hemstitching has been part of fine embroideries in many cultures. Table textiles often feature these techniques. Extend them to other weavings. Note the hem in the Ukrainian linen panel shown on figure 2-70. It was richly embroidered with cross stitch. A row of hemstitching

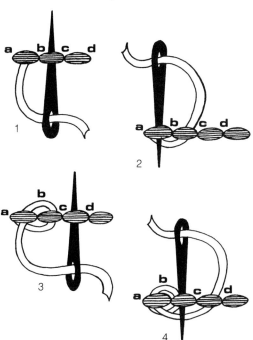

2-68. Pekinese stitch. The first pass and base of this stitch is a row of even backstitches. In the second pass, backstitches are threaded in the sequence shown in the drawing, forward and back. Keep tension even and the threading stitch relaxed, making small circles or loops.

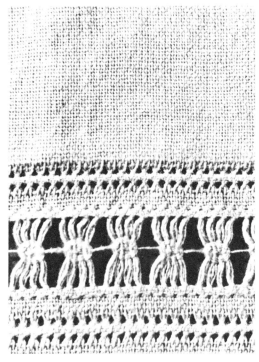

2-69. The wide border of drawn-thread embroidery on a linen tunic is placed above the hemline. This piece was embroidered on the loom. The neck edge is shown in figure 2-12. (Woven and photographed by Penelope B. Drooker; from *Embroidering with the Loom* by Penelope B. Drooker)

then a border design is worked on the deep hem. Note the whole design, with everything carefully complete, including the square corner with a cross stitch design. The hem is folded and sewn just below the hemstitched row. It is an excellent example of total design. This is just one of dozens of exquisitely embroidered panels, cushions, coats, dresses, and church cloths made by Mrs. Kuchman in the traditional Ukrainian stitches and patterns. The colors are fresh and lovely—blue, red, and yellow on white linen.

2-70. Ukrainian wall panel, with embroidered and hemstitched hem. The corner is especially well designed and worked. (Embroiderer, Mrs. Kuchman, Chicago, Illinois)

More Hemming Ideas

An elegant finish for a hem on a handwoven silk dress is wide lace binding, sewn flat over the stitched edge. It not only looks pretty but serves the useful purpose of covering the edge of the single turned hem as well. Tussah silk cut edges ravel easily, so a close zigzag should be stitched along the edge. The close stitch will make a ridge in places, which shows when the hem is hand-sewn. The remedy: hand-sew a 1¼-inch (unfolded) nylon lace seam binding just below the stitching; then the heaviest-stitched edge ridges are cut as the other edge of the binding is sewn to the dress. The result is a smooth hem on the right side, a secure and neatly covered edge on the inside. On the right of figure 2-71 note that the side seams are zigzagged with a more open stitch which does not pucker and ridge the edge.

A tabard of Guatemalan handloomed cotton (figure 2-72) is finished with a wide hem across the bottom and along the sides. At the bottom, the edge is turned in and hemmed. Along the side, the selvedge is hemmed without a turn. The mitered corner is neat and flat. This kind of a hem is a good choice for finishing table textiles such as placemats, cloths, or runners.

2-71. Wide nylon lace binding is sewn above and below the covered cut edge of the hem on a silk dress. There is no visible line of hemming on the right side.

2-72. Wide hem with mitered corners on a tabard of Guatemalan cotton.

Integral Finishes

As weavers, we have a prime opportunity to design some finishes as part of the process. Exploit the possibilities of the craft rather than always using the customary sewing methods, trying to bend them to fit the sometimes unusual needs of handwoven textiles. Several of these special methods have developed or have been observed while putting this book together, and the following are just examples of what can be found in other sections of this book.

Show both sides of a weave. When the two faces of a textile are different, turn or roll the hem to the top side. It looks like an added binding. There is no bulk from sewing on. The color and pattern are related, and you have an integral trim.

The corners of a narrow bookmark, shown in figure 2-74, have a shaped hem end. The pattern of the weaving suggests a pointed finish. The

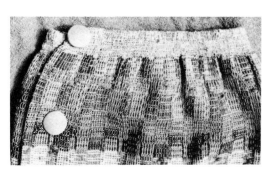

2-73. Wefts are pulled to form the skirt band and slightly gather the skirt. (Weaver, Joan Walker, Renton, Washington)

Fullness is eased in and a waist band is formed by drawing up the wefts along the top of a skirt (figure 2-73). This is an outstanding solution to the problem of a bunchy skirt band on handwoven yardage. The width of the skirt should be carefully planned in relation to the amount that it has to come in at the waist so that the gathers are not too bulky. It can be done on a skirt that is tapered in at the top. Any time you can accomplish a better fit without adding on seams and pieces a total design emerges. See figure 5-20 for another view of this long skirt.

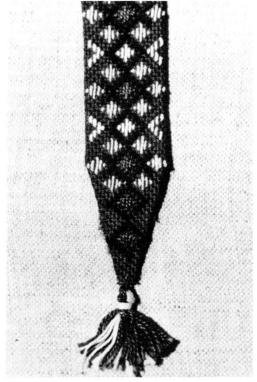

2-74. A bookmark woven in Greece has the corners folded back into a pointed end with a tassel. A sash idea?

corners are folded back and a tassel completes the end. A grosgrain ribbon is glued to the back and stiffens the band of red, white, and black pearl thread.

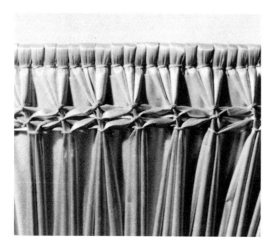

2-75. Overlaid and sewn edge on a basket from Italy.

2-76. A smashing edge idea on a basket of bentwood and splints.

Weavers always look at baskets (and own them)! The basket edge in figure 2-75, on a small basket from Italy, might adapt to a textile. It has glossy reeds overlaid on the outside and brought up and over the edge. This pattern of catching groups together or laying on threads may give you an idea. Try couching or a soumak technique. An open-weave edge on a basket of rough bentwood and splints (figure 2-76) suggests an interesting edge design that could be duplicated on a woven edge with needle stitches.

Traditional Hemming Methods to Try

- Plain hemming, with an overcast stitch. Stitches might show on the other side.
- Blind-hemming. Stitches pick up one thread of the weave and are further apart than in plain hemming. They should not show much on the right side.
- Slipstitch. This is inconspicuous from either side as the stitch is run inside of the fold and only one thread of fabric is picked up (figure 3-8).
- Rolled hem. Gently rolled hems, not turned and creased, are traditionally found on finest lawn or linen handkerchiefs, handmade lingerie, and sheer materials like chiffon. They are sewn with tiny slipstitches or overcast, or are sometimes blind-hemmed. The rolled hem may be turned to the inside or rolled up to the topside and sewn with embroidery stitches.

Edges and ends lead you directly to seams and joinings—in the following chapter.

3. Joins and Seams

Any two pieces of cloth fastened together are joined. The join is usually called a seam. The word *joining*, or *join*, as used here, usually means decorative or noticeable stitches, woven-in ties, loops, or slits that are a part of a join. It is an obvious seaming that becomes a trim or embellishment and an important part of the planned design. The word *seam*, as used here, is mostly reserved for the more conventional methods of machine-stitching or hand-sewing pieces together, usually in a less conspicuous way. However, double topstitching, for instance, can be subtle but decorative, too.

This chapter is for stitchers, embroiderers, and sewers as well as for weavers. We all work with fabric and fibers, often joining two or more sections together. Artisans are blending and recognizing all fiber techniques and methods, with weavers learning embroidery stitches and embroiderers learning to weave. The fiber world is wide open, with imaginary fences down. There is so much to say, to explore, and learn about joinings!

The need for joinings evolved in primitive cultures because their narrow looms produced cloth that was too narrow to wear or to use for coverings or windscreens. Joining two or more sections of cloth to create a larger unit is an old device applied to utilize products of a narrow loom.

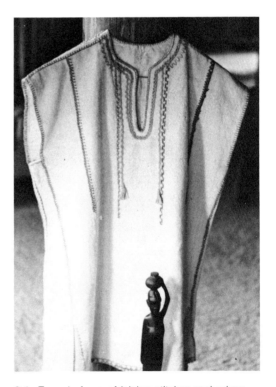

3-1. Tour de force of joining stitches and edges. This reference/sampler is on an African country cloth tunic. Three-inch-wide strips are sewn together for a garment of wearable size.

3-2. Velvet patches and embroidered seams on a well-designed wallhanging. Note the fabric tab hangers over the stained dowel. (Artist, Jill Nordfors, Gig Harbor, Washington; photograph by Beverly Rush)

Kente cloth from Ghana, woven in strips only a few inches wide, must be joined to make their voluminous robes. Mexican huipiles are composed of narrow lengths joined in many combinations of two or more sections. These are only two examples of large textiles assembled from narrow ones. A study of ethnic costumes and textiles provides a wealth of ideas, with joining methods in use everywhere. These tech-

niques and methods apply to household and decorative articles as well as to clothing.

Thrifty use of worn clothing and new scraps from sewing led to patchwork and crazy quilts of rich materials with embroidered seams; today, these are planned and expertly stitched and embellished, of new materials, raising the craft of our great-grandmother's to new heights.

While we now have multiple choices of using various loom widths or wide, ready-woven cloth to work with, combining small units into large is a challenge that allows for great variety and inventiveness. We cut and sew, fabricate and weave to size, and assemble and combine. We hand-sew, machine-stitch, crochet, tie, or lace pieces of cloth together, using any and all suitable methods. We speak here mostly of hand-sewn seams. Decorative machine-stitching is another fascinating aspect—another study.

TECHNIQUES AND METHODS

The basic techniques necessary are hand needlework, machine-sewing, or both: machine-sewing for strength and handwork for strength as well as for a truly handcrafted result. Hand-sewn seams, satisfactory for eons before the sewing machine was invented, appear in garments and other textiles from other cultures. Often the sewing is crudely done, apparently with no thought of continuing the exquisite craftsmanship found in the fabric itself. Sometimes the sewing-up is done by children or members of the group who are less expert. Hand-picked seams are a hallmark of fine tailoring. On handwoven material, especially on a heavy wool or crisp linen, they serve to flatten the seam or hem, adding a hand-stitched look. Topstitched seams by machine accomplish about the same thing, but "by hand" has more distinction.

TOTAL DESIGN

While you are planning to combine widths and shapes, think total design. Weavers have the options of choosing the loom, yarns, colors, and weaving method beforehand. Stitchers begin with carefully selected textiles. The solutions for both then become about the same. The basic techniques necessary are needlework and machine-sewing. Total design—to me—means thinking through from the beginning to the end product in use. Will it be worn and washed—or hang passively on a wall? Will it have abrasive wear, or be lifted and handled often? Does the complete design call for a decorative joining of the parts or an inconspicuous one that does the work of holding the cloth together, quietly?

The proposed use of the textile and it's weight, weave, and type all help to determine the method of seaming. For example, in order to eliminate bulk on heavy cloth with seams just brought together, not overlapped, a hand-sewn stitch that does a real joining is needed (figure 2-66).

The designed joining can be a major part of the piece and express the total concept. Often a matching thread will add richness and texture where a contrasting color might not be just right.

Strongly contrasting colors may be the perfect solution for another piece. Visible, needed machine-stitching can be covered with a hand-stitch, or can be simply threaded with a heavier or more colorful thread: effective but not intrusive.

My own preference and practice is to seam by hand. I like the control possible, especially on a loose or a heavy weave. Some years ago, when yards and yards of drapery were custom-handwoven, I always hand-seamed and hemmed them, using the same yarns as those in the weaving. Usually a moderately decorative stitch was used, often worked on both sides of the seam so the join was attractive when seen from the "wrong" side. It was worth the extra effort to follow through with the extra touch on a totally designed product.

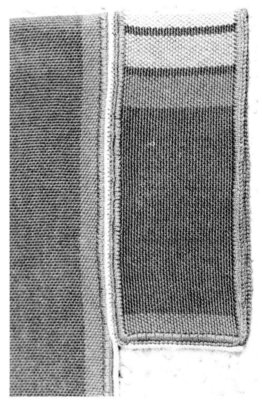

3-3. A total design—precise and perfectly crafted join and edge with a thoughtful color plan. The line of white is a smart touch. The edge finish and joining are crocheted in the same pearl cotton as the weave. This geometric tunic uses a narrow rectangle joined to the main rectangle to form a cap sleeve. (Weaver, Jean Sullivan, Seattle, Washington)

3-4. Curly mohair helps to camouflage the sleeve seam in a coat woven and sewn by Clara Chapman, Orcas Island, Washington. The butted selvedges are slip-stitched. (Photograph by Kent Kammerer)

Decisions before Weaving

Preparation for joins or seams made on the loom can help a great deal when the combining is done off the loom. Whenever possible, work an edge finish or a joining edge on the loom while the fabric is in tension for side seams, slits at sides, front edges on a garment, or as part of the joining along seams and edges. Loom plans should include some of the following, to enhance or add to the join. Decide if:

- edge warps should be finer, coarser, other colors
- pattern border is to be threaded in
- a closer or wider sett is needed at the edge
- a guideline of contrasting, doubled or heavier warp should be put in to help place a needlework row as a border or part of the join
- a needle stitch, such as buttonhole, will be worked along the edge as the weaving progresses as a base for crochet, lacing stitches, or other method
- selvedge will be left plain for a butted seam and needs to be especially even and well-woven for that purpose
- loops should be woven along the edge for later lacing, crochet, or needlework stitch joining
- long loops or cut ends for a tied join are required
- loops for buttonholes, to be chained, twisted, buttonholed, or wrapped, are necessary
- slits woven for buttonholes, lacing, ties, etc., can be used
- extensions, such as tabs woven as part of a join are a solution
- surface textures along the edges will be woven as a border to hide the joining, such as picked-up loops or Ghiordes knots

Selecting Stitches

Choosing the most appropriate joining stitch is an important first step. To widen your vocabulary of techniques and methods, learn to look at embroidery stitches carefully—diagrams as well as finished work. See if the stitch can do the necessary straddling of a seam and become a join, such as Sorbello stitch (figure 3-5). Experiment with cloth and thread. Try many versions and adaptations. Some stitches are natural joiners. Others are best reserved for surface and edge uses. Just about any stitch that begins with threads laid down as a first step, such as the raised chain band (figures 3-31 and 3-32), can be used to join. Others are the large family of fagotting stitches. Cross stitches in myriad variations or blanket/buttonhole stitch, which is worked along each edge, then whipped, laced or crocheted together, can also be used. The list goes on, and I will leave you to relish the excitement of some discoveries for yourselves! Drawings and examples of some especially useful and attractive stitches follow later in this chapter.

Proportion

When a decorative stitch is planned for joining seams, think about the width of the seam in proportion to the rest of the piece, especially in clothing. A wide, heavy stitch and yarn on a lightweight garment will seem coarse and not as harmonious as a narrow, finer stitch. On a large flowing wool poncho made of handspun

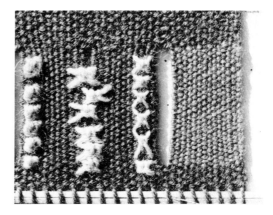

3-5. Sorbello stitch on edges and as a join, from the scroll.

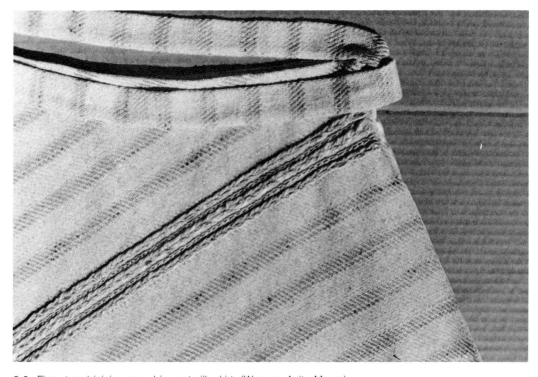

3-6. Five-strand joining on a bias-cut silk skirt. (Weaver, Anita Mayer)

yarn, an inch-wide seam stitch of the same yarn would be appropriate. A fine cotton jacket would benefit from a narrow seam stitched with fine cotton. The proportion of seam to weaving is a consideration with other products as well. On joined units for a rug or on sections of drapery, for example, the band of joining stitches may be planned as the major emphasis and may be of large scale, with good effect. Admittedly, there are usually exceptions! The five-strand joining on the skirt in figure 3-6 (also figure 3-52) is wide but was planned to be the main feature, quite dramatically designed to emphasize the diagonal cut and woven stripes of the skirt. But do consider proportion and suitability here, as you do with all of your designing.

To Summarize

A few hints:

- Machine-stitch with matching thread to firm a bias cut, to keep edges from raveling, and for necessary strength.
- Enhance visible stitching with a needle stitch.
- One or more rows of machine-stitching will act as guidelines for hand-stitching. They will be hidden and will give strength.
- A cut edge can be folded back, pressed, and ready for a covering stitch to join.
- A well-woven selvedge can be joined as is, with no turnback.
- A cut edge may have to be folded into a hem, pressed, then basted or pinned. A basting can either be removed later or remain, if hidden.

I hope that this brief skimming of a big subject will give you some ideas and point you in new directions. Summon all of your best instincts for suitability, original use of stitches, and good design—then combine them with knowledgeable and careful craftsmanship. The result will be a true expression of the complete artisan.

SEAMS

Directions and methods for sewing conventional seams are readily found in the many good general books on sewing. Ideas and methods given here are especially suitable for handwoven clothing and household textiles. Often, an unconventional method serves the purpose and seems right for

a particular product. One of the options for handweavers is that of shaping the sections so that most of the edges are selvedges.

Classic Methods of Seaming

The conventional machine-stitched seam, with right sides together then stitched, is universally used. The raw edges can be bound with tape, overcast by hand, buttonholed, or turned back about one-quarter of an inch, deep enough to prevent fraying. To flatten the seam, topstitch along both sides, preferably by hand. The classic French seam is stitched together once, with wrong sides together, and then stitched again, with the right sides together. There are no raw edges, but it is bulky for wool or for a heavy weave; it is best used on lightweight or loosely woven cloth. Other types of seams to look for are whipped, flat-felled, and double topstitched.

Two seams that are especially suitable for handwovens, the butted seam and the lapped seam, can be quite showy or inconspicuous and are trim and smooth. The butted seam consists of two pieces just meeting. Weavers prefer it, and it lends itself to joining stitches, without extra thickness and bulk. It can be very flat where two selvedges meet. Examples are shown throughout the book, but note especially figure 3-29. The butted seam is joined with a Rumanian stitch. If edges are turned back with raw edges protected, then the two edges just brought together, the joining is on the fold of each edge. In all seams, matching color and inconspicuous stitches will minimize the join. In textured textiles, the seams will almost disappear.

In the lapped seam, one edge is put over the other. This seam is neatest when both edges are selvedge. When one edge is selvedge and the other cut, lap so that the selvedge edge is on top (figure 3-7).

3-7. A rectangular tunic of pearl cotton is sewn down the sides with a lapped seam. A wide stripe was woven at the selvedges, and the overlap is just the width of the stripe. Sewn inconspicuously, the edges of the armhole and the slit at the bottom are the even selvedges. No added stitches were necessary. The square neckline and the hemline are edged with a solid, fine crochet stitch in the same pearl cotton. (Weaver, Jean Sullivan)

THE LOOK OF JOINS AND SEAMS

Seams or joins can be very showy or hardly noticeable. Apart from the several methods of seaming on a sewing machine, there is a whole world of joinings to work by hand. Inconspicuous, elaborate, or moderately fancy—thoughtfully choose your method.

Almost Invisible Seams

These are used when you want the two edges to blend in and be unobtrusive. To make subtle joins, use a matching yarn. Carefully align the two pieces to be joined, so that the weft rows follow straight across. Finally, put a straight, horizontal stitch in so it looks like a continuation of the weft. A pattern weave will make this a little easier, but, with care, it can be very satisfactory on a plain weave. This method of straight stitches following the weft rows is useful in seaming a tablecloth, bedspread, or straight side seams in a garment, where the join is not a feature and the seam is to be inconspicuous.

On curved or bias sections, the results will not be as inconspicuous, and in that case the solution would be to use a stitch that will show as part of the design.

Two unobtrusive joining stitches used in past years on loom-width strips joined for bed sheets are the slip stitch and the ancient, or antique, stitch. The slip stitch (figure 3-8) is especially suitable for use when joining two selvedge edges. At the selvedge, pick up one or two wefts at a time. The ancient stitch is a little more noticeable than the slip stitch. It consists of slanting or straight stitches taken from side to side across the seam (figure 3-9).

Woven Seams

A truly weaverly joining, smooth and flat, results when the weft ends are woven in from edge to edge, so it looks as if the material was not seamed at all. Figure 3-10 shows an example in progress. There are at least two ways to weave the join. Wefts can be extended during the weaving, then woven in from side to side. Another, if feasible, is to cut the selvedge off and remove enough

of the warps until the weft ends are long enough to thread into a needle and weave in. If you plan to do this, be sure to have a weaving width that is wide enough to be cut back. To keep the outside warps from "floating," clip just an inch or so of the edge, weave those wefts in, then clip, weave, and so on. With mohair or a clingy yarn, there should be no trouble with raveling while you weave the seam. Whichever scheme is followed, the sequence of the main weaving must be kept, from side to side, and the tension of the woven ends should match all across.

To weave in, clamp or weight the two sections of cloth at the top of the seam close together. Lay the wefts back and weave in alternately from side to side. Keep the wefts in the exact order of the weaving sequence. Weave into the adjoining edge for about an inch. The distance will depend upon the kind and size of yarn and how firmly it is woven, but the wefts should be woven in far enough so they will not pull out with wear. The ends can be clipped close or left in a short fringe, which can be on either the outside or inside. Follow the weave, over and under, whether it is a pattern or plain weave.

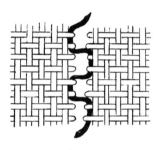

3-8. Slip stitch, an inconspicuous joining stitch, was used on the coat shown in figure 3-4.

3-9. Ancient, or antique, stitch, worked with straight or slanting stitches from edge to edge.

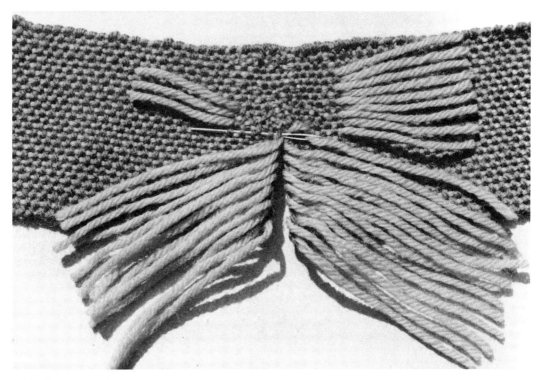

3-10. Woven seam in progress.

A Look at Directions

When writing directions, I always hesitate to put in too many specific hand and finger positions. It can be confusing and may prevent someone from doing it the most comfortable way. In the workshops, there are usually one or two left-handers who have to transpose the directions; in our mostly right-handed world, I bow to them in respect for how well they cheerfully cope!

STITCHES

Embroidery has been a part of my life since earliest memory. My mother always enhanced our clothing and household items—from curtains to tablecloths to towels—with lovely stitches. As soon as I could hold a needle and poke it through cloth, my enchantment with stitches was set for life! When weaving became a prime interest, embroidery simply became an extension of it and went beyond surface embellishment.

Results of my own experimentation and analysis of stitches are reflected in the choice of stitches presented as joining stitches. Most of them are considered and used as surface or edge stitches, but they can also be adapted to be joiners. There are many more, as you will discover in your own study of stitches. Take a stitch and work it every way you can. Extend the "arms" and the "legs" to different lengths. Place stitches up close or far apart. Combine stitches. The only "rule" is to work the stitch correctly and to let it keep it's own characteristic look. For example, if the Sorbello stitch hitches are cinched down tightly, or it is worked small in a very fine thread, the puffy little square is lost, along with the reason you might have chosen to work the stitch in the first place (figure 3-34). Open, closed, fine, coarse, large, or small—try variations of all, but within the characteristics of the stitch. Many stitches have "edge" as part of their name. Don't let that stop you from using them as a join or in other ways.

As I was finishing the assembly of this section, when all examples and drawings of stitches were at hand, I was quite surprised to see that the majority of my illustrations of joins and stitches happened to be on clothing. Do keep in mind that all of these stitches can be and have been used on household and decorative textiles as well.

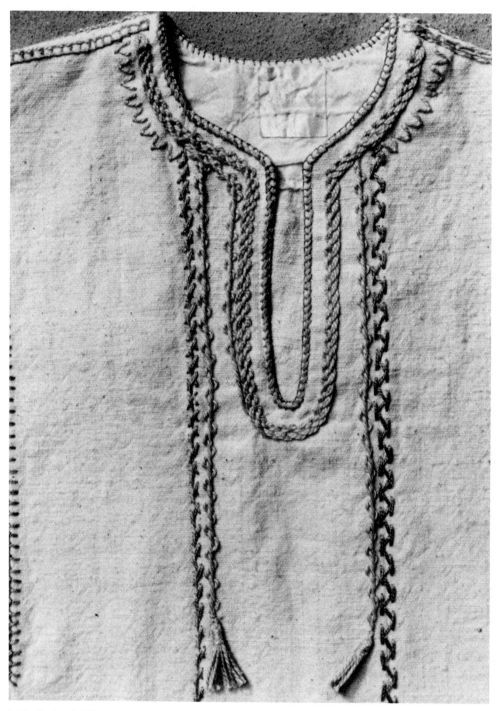

3-11. Tunic of African handwoven country cloth, with all seams and edges embroidered with joining and edge stitches. The details of the stitches are shown in figures 3-12 through 3-18.

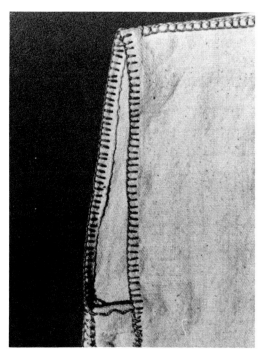

3-12. Buttonhole and variations, raised chain band on the seam, right.

3-14. Neckline back: whipped buttonhole, Palestrina, and velvet stitches at the center, Y at sides; seams worked in raised chain band, at left, and laced running stitch, at right; two tassels.

3-13. Eskimo lacing, two sizes, on hem and right edge; buttonhole rows facing each other, left edge.

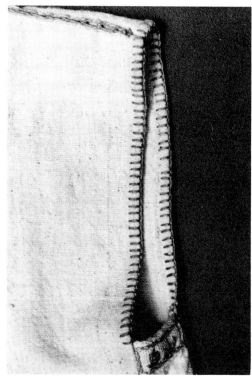

3-15. Armhole edges, buttonhole stitch; whipped chain on shoulder seam; monogram at bottom.

Joins and Seams 69

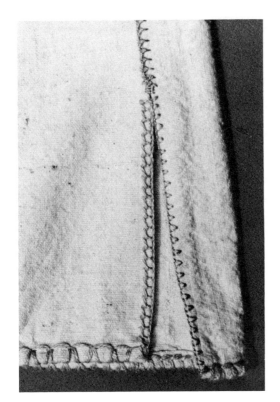

3-16. Slits at hemline; whipped buttonhole at left; slanted blanket stitch at right; Eskimo lacing at hem.

3-17. More buttonhole variations, left and right at slit; Eskimo lacing, two sizes, at hem and at left.

Joining and Edge Stitches

A teaching aid for joining and edge stitches, a sleeveless tunic top from Africa, turned into a tour de force of stitches on every seam and every edge (figures 3-11 through 3-18). It is composed of handwoven white cotton "country cloth." Yards of narrow strips, from about two inches to five inches in width, are woven then coiled into great wheels for the market. These strips are later machine-stitched into loose and comfortable tunic tops. With twelve seams and many edges, the top is a perfect showcase for joining stitches and edge finishes. All of the stitches are in several shades of cobalt blue, in stranded floss, pearl 3 and 5. The top is now a walking, wearable example of stitches—another reference/sampler.

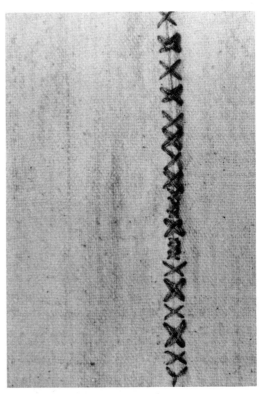

3-18. Detail of joining stitch: cross stitch and cross stitch flower; one Y stitch at the bottom.

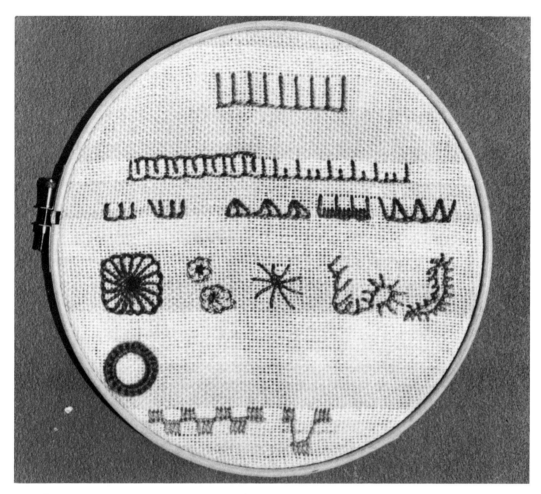

3-19. Buttonhole/blanket stitch variations for a reference/sampler on a hoop.

Seventeen different stitches, plus variations, are used, some as edge finishes. Several are worked in variations of size, spacing, or threads. Some are combinations, such as threaded or laced running stitches. And there are six variations of blanket/buttonhole stitch! A few small tassels and a monogram were thrown in for good measure. Perhaps this exercise will give you an idea of the fun of working stitches.

Blanket/Buttonhole Stitch

Blanket stitch and buttonhole stitch (figure 3-19) are interchangeable terms—in general usage. In fact, there is some historical difference. Blanket stitch was the edge stitch on blankets, worked in several combinations of long and short vertical stitch groups; one was three stitches together, slanting to the center in a triangular shape. Since the basic path of the thread in blanket stitch is also the one taken by the buttonhole stitch, and the buttonhole stitch is worked in closed or open fashion (with numerous variations of knotting, detached stitches, and groupings), it is now accepted that the terms blanket stitch and buttonhole stitch mean the same.

In any case, it is an edge or joining stitch.

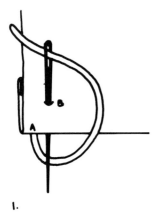

I.

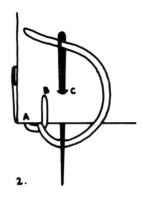

2.

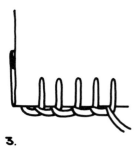

3.

3-20. Buttonhole/blanket stitch as an edge. For a joining, work it horizontally.

The drawing in figure 3-20 shows it as an edge stitch. It is often and easily used as a joining stitch by placing the two edges butted together or overlapped (figure 3-21). For a join, work the stitch horizontally, from left to right. As an edge stitch, it is the preparation for a crocheted, laced, or whipped join.

The true tailor's buttonhole stitch (figure 3-22) does have a difference in the structure, although, again, the path of the thread is essentially the buttonhole/blanket stitch. For a tailored buttonhole, it is worked over a laid thread, with an extra twist in the stitch, which makes a firm little knot along the edge. This, in turn, is similar to the plaited edge stitch (figure 3-23). The extra twist and small knot add to the tightness and wear and is recommended for covering rings for lacing (figure 5-13), for edges that need more strength from the stitch, and where you might want the knotted edge for looks. Except when it is used on a buttonhole, it does not have to be worked over a laid thread.

3-21. Buttonhole stitch sews lapped seam and edge on a linen skirt.

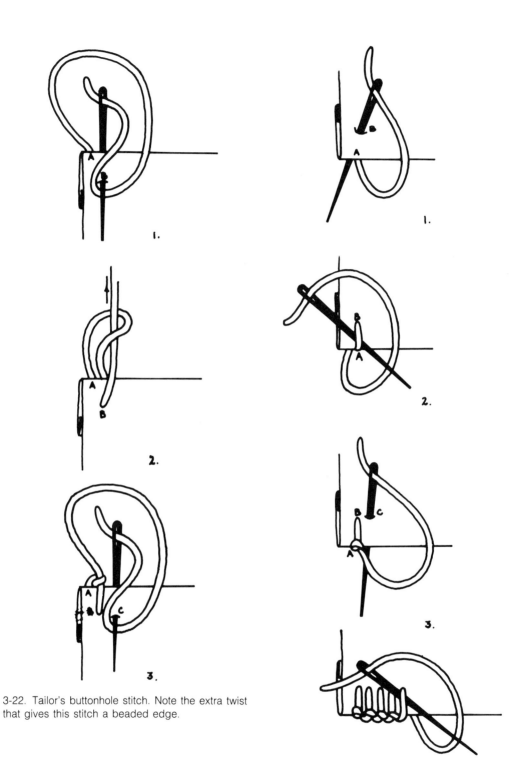

3-22. Tailor's buttonhole stitch. Note the extra twist that gives this stitch a beaded edge.

3-23. Plaited edge stitch. Note that the result is much the same as the tailor's buttonhole, but the method is different.

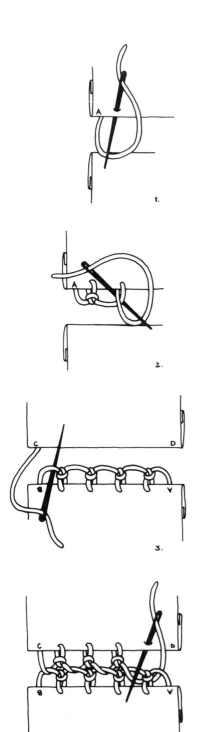

1.

2.

3.

4.

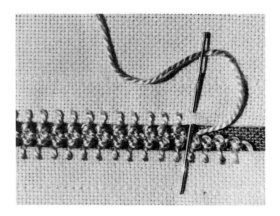

3-25. Antwerp edging stitch in progress. Here it is used as a joining stitch.

3-24. Antwerp edging stitch, or detached knotted buttonhole stitch. While this is called an edging stitch and a detached surface stitch, it works very well as a joining stitch, as seen in figure 3-25.

The Antwerp edging stitch (figures 3-24, 3-25) adapts naturally as a joining stitch when worked along one edge, then on the opposite edge. The join is made as each stitch is looped around the opposite one (figure 3-25). This forms a twist between the knots and a full, textured line results. It fills the space between edges. Try it as just an edging stitch, too, following 1 and 2 in the diagram. It is also known as the detached knotted buttonhole stitch. Try this stitch related to the buttonhole stitch. It serves the same purposes as the more familiar stitch, but adds it's own dimension. The extra twist or knot increases the richness and interest of surface embroidery, edges and joins.

Combining Stitches

Combining stitches is another fascinating and very rewarding pursuit. An excellent example is on the edges and joining of a reversible Welsh tapestry coat by Eleanor Van de Water (figure 3-26). The base stitch of the wide joining band is buttonhole stitch with two rows of chain stitch worked over it. This detail shows the joining stitches at the sides and the added length at the bottom. A rather tricky problem was solved perfectly here. Because the coat is reversible, the joinings had to look right on both sides. Also, the stitches used exactly repeat those on the edges all around, unifying the whole garment, inside and outside. See how neatly the corner is worked, where edge and join blend together. Also see figures 2-25 and 2-26.

3-26. Welsh tapestry reversible coat, detail. Joining and edge stitches are the same on both sides. A strip is added to extend the length. Also see figures 2-25 and 2-26. (Designer/stitcher, Eleanor Van de Water, Vancouver, Washington; photograph by Eleanor Van de Water)

Closed Cretan Stitch

This stitch, usually used as a surface stitch, is very popular with weavers as a joining stitch, either solid and full, or open and loose (figure 3-27). The first stitch (figure 3-28)—A to B and up at C—is like the Rumanian stitch with just one catch-down, but it continues with two catch-down stitches, forming a cross-over in the center. The two edges can meet so there is no space between, or they can be spread apart. It can be worked over a closed seam, along an edge, or as an embellishment—curving and with stitches of different lengths. Note the position of the needle at each step, and whether the stitch is worked from left or right, vertically or horizontally.

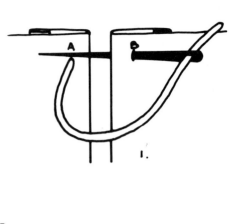

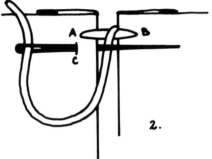

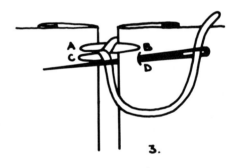

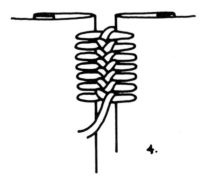

3-27. Closed cretan stitch joins two sections of a huipil of the Chinantec Indians, Mexico. (Courtesy, Leslie Grace, La Tienda, Seattle, Washington)

3-28. Closed cretan stitch as a joining.

Rumanian Stitch

The Rumanian stitch is another most satisfactory stitch for a join (figure 3-29). It is easily worked, closes firmly, and can be narrow and unobtrusive or bold and wide and colorful. It is similar to the closed cretan stitch but has just the one catch-down in the center. Perhaps better known to embroiderers as the Rumanian couching stitch, it joins as well. While trying all ways to weave columns as alternates to plain wrapping, the wrap-and-split method evolved. It is a woven version of the Rumanian embroidery stitch (figure 2-57).

To work this stitch, follow the letters in figure 3-30 and notice the needle positions. The stitch can be worked either sideways or up and down. Besides joining and couching, it is an adaptable stitch for surfaces, straight lines, or free stitching.

3-29. Detail of Rumanian stitch joining at the shoulder of a vest. Note the wide crocheted edge around the neckline. Other stitches for embellishment are outline, Y, Pekinese, and single chain stitch.

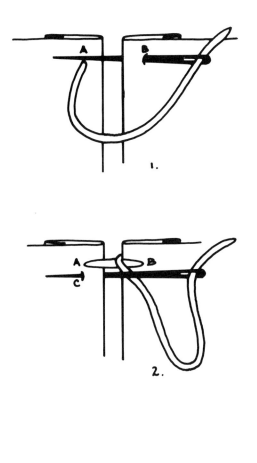

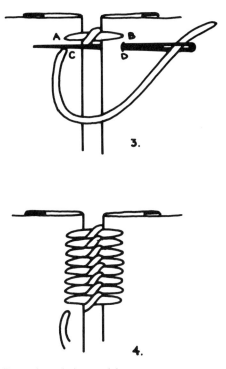

3-30. Rumanian stitch as a join.

Raised Chain Band

The raised chain band stitch is a good joiner and is decorative, too (figure 3-31). It is worked from the top down in two passes. The raised band effect is heightened by the use of two colors or shades for the two parts and this varies it considerably. On the reference/sampler tunic (figure 3-14), light and darker blue were used. The rounded band accents a line as a surface stitch or as a join. It can curve and have stitches of varied sizes. The bar stitches can be completely covered or show along the edge. The center loop stitch can be toward one side so that the straight stitches show unequal lengths. The loops, centered, completely cover the seam line or space. Use it as a join on ponchos, bedspreads, pillows or as a border or edging on clothing. Use cotton floss, pearl, linen, or wool yarns.

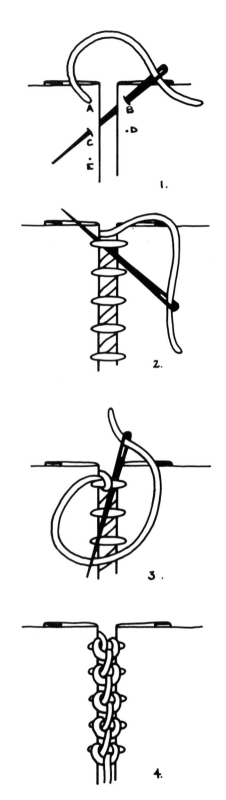

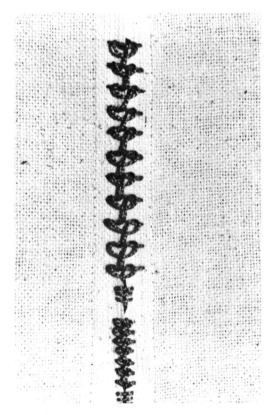

3-31. Example of raised chain band stitch as a join. It also works well as a surface or edging stitch.

3-32. Raised chain band as a joining stitch.

Follow figure 3-32 to work this stitch. Place the two edges close together, weighting or pinning them to a firm surface. (1) Lay the foundation bars from edge to edge, straight stitches evenly spaced and of even length (see (1) A, B, C of the drawing); the knotted thread begins inside the hem and comes through from the back. (2) The loop stitch begins at the back, also. Anchor the chain thread to the bar by going under it and up to the left. Snug this stitch to the bar, without pulling or distorting it. (3) Make a buttonhole or "Y" stitch loop, coming out over the loop to catch it down, and ready to repeat the under, up-to-the-left and loop sequence. (4) These are the completed stitches. The loop stitch does not go through the cloth. The reverse side is a row of slanting straight stitches from the bar stitch.

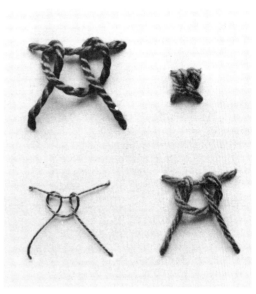

3-34. An expanded view of the Sorbello stitch, in various sizes of yarn and stitch.

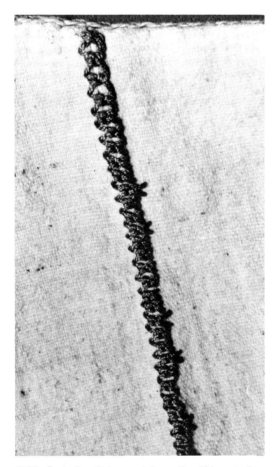

3-33. Sorbello stitch as a join on the African tunic. An occasional stitch has the bars brought out to the sides.

The top example in figure 3-31 is of large open stitches of pearl 5 to show the path of the thread. A small, tighter version below it shows how a firm join would be made. It is worked on cloth with unturned selvedge edges (the drawing shows it on turned-back hems).

Sorbello Stitch

This stitch is such a favorite it has almost become a trademark! It performs well as a joining stitch (figure 3-33) but also as a deep-textured surface stitch in borders or geometric designs. Originating in Sorbello, Italy, one use was on pillow covers; colorful geometric patterns and figures were embroidered on loosely woven cotton. It readily adapts as a join because it is a square (figure 3-35), with all four corners anchored (at A–B and C–D) and bridging a seam. Close together, the squares will completely cover the space. Many variations come with the legs and arms of different lengths (figures 3-34 and 3-5). This little stitch has endless design possibilities. It curves and skips over spaces. Try giant stitches with several hitches in large and multiple strands of yarn.

The stitch (figure 3-35) is composed of two hitches, hung on a bar, with anchoring stitches at each of the four corners. The reverse side has just one diagonal stitch, B to C, so most of the yarn is on the surface. Follow the letters and needle positions in the drawing. Note that at the second hitch, the thread is over the loop to hold it down. Drawing number 4 shows the start of the next stitch directly below, at C, as worked in a vertical line. When worked horizontally as a join, from left to right, the bar A–B is on one edge, crossing down to the other edge, C and D, and the diagonal stitch is the only join. This is not as firm as the vertical method, but joins adequately. When a continuous line of stitches is to be worked from left to right, the second stitch will start one thread from B, or in the same hole. To vary the placement of the hitches, relax the bar enough so it is pulled to different levels.

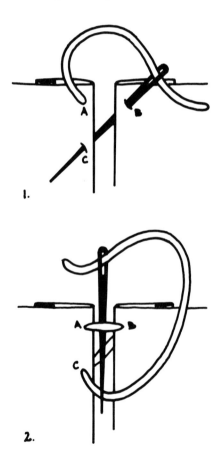

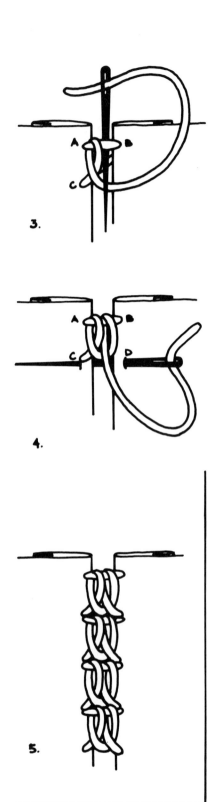

3-35. Sorbello stitch as a join.

Closed Herringbone Stitch

This stitch bridges the space and fastens two pieces of cloth together. The edges can just meet, or they can overlap. Be warned, however, that the closed herringbone stitch does use up a lot of yarn. About 80 yards—nearly all of two 40-yard hanks of needlepoint wool—were used up working this stitch on a knee-length wool coat.

To work this stitch (figure 3-36) place the two edges close together. Work from left to right. Start *A* (knot inside of the hem) from the back and close to the edge nearest you. Take the thread up to the other edge, to *B*, out at *C*, then cross over, down to *D*, out at *E*, ready to make stitch two. In closed fashion, the stitches are placed as close together as possible. In an open or wider stitch, the next stitch is set over. For the best result as a joining stitch, a solid line of stitches is made. The drawing shows space between edges for clarity, but in a tight join the edges should meet. Number 6 in the drawing shows the closed herringbone along a hem, set a little lower than in figure 2-62.

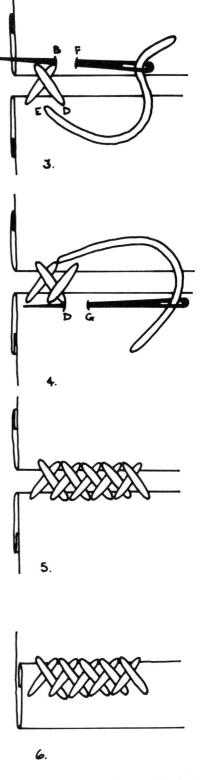

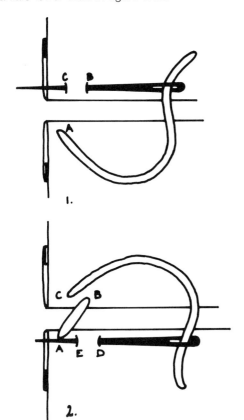

3-36. Closed herringbone stitch as a join. In *6* it is shown on a hem.

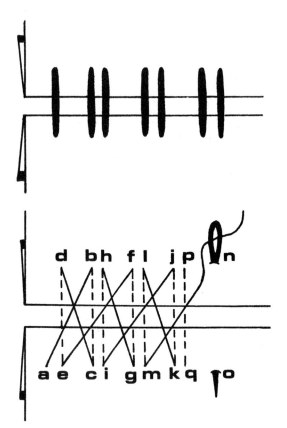

3-37. The basket stitch as a joining stitch, showing both back (top) and front (bottom). A firm join, the straight stitches at the back connect and reinforce the stitch.

Basket Stitch

Basket stitch . . . Slav cross stitch . . . plait stitch . . . long-armed or long-legged cross stitch—call this stitch what you will, they are all related, with minor differences in placement of stitches. As with a number of stitches that have been around for a long time, there is a conflict of names. Basket stitch (figure 3-37), basket edge stitch (figure 2-26), and plaited edge stitch (figure 3-23) differ somewhat, but sometimes the two basket stitches are called plaited. To add to the confusion, the basket stitches look like the herringbone stitch on the top side. But you can tell from the back which stitch it is because herringbone has horizontal stitches and basket has vertical or slanted stitches.

Although basket stitch is categorized as a surface stitch, especially rich for borders, I have added it to my group of joining stitches because

it makes a firm and full join. Worked from left to right, horizontally, with very close stitches, it fills the space and holds two sections of cloth together handsomely and well.

The drawing in figure 3-37 shows pairs of straight stitches on the back for a stable join. When set over a few threads to the right, the stitches will be slanted on the back. Follow the letters carefully, and notice that the stitches are taken forward and backward. For a very close, solid join, place the stitches in the holes of the previous stitch so they will crowd in. I suggest you practice this stitch on a sampling cloth, varying the height and width and closeness of the stitches, because it is a bit confusing at first. Once mastered, though, it moves right along.

"Bonus" Stitches

While choosing and working embroidery stitches for this book, and trying out adaptations to use as joins and in different ways, I found that some stitches that were worked for a top-side effect provided a first pass for another stitch on the reverse side. Several of these happenings grew into a small list of stitches to use when a reversible or two-sided embroidery was wanted.

For example, a surprise occurred when stitches were chosen to edge, hem, and embellish the linen vest shown in figure 2-64. Closed herringbone stitches on the hem, inside, created two rows of backstitch on the top side. Coincidentally, the Pekinese stitch (figure 2-68) was planned for the top-side edge; it requires a first pass of even backstitches—and there they were! The one row of herringbone provided two rows of backstitch for two rows of Pekinese stitch, resulting in a full, rich border.

Another example, open cretan stitch, when worked along an edge, becomes an over-the-edge stitch when the stitches on the back are whipped, duplicating the cretan stitch on the front.

Another surprise was the plush or velvet stitch (figure 3-38). Experimentation to see if this surface texture stitch could be woven produced a two-sided textile with a looped surface on one side and cut pile on the other.

As a needle stitch with continuous thread, there will be no surface ends on the reverse side, just two rows of running stitch. And here we go again, with a pair of first passes for threaded running, a loose version of Pekinese

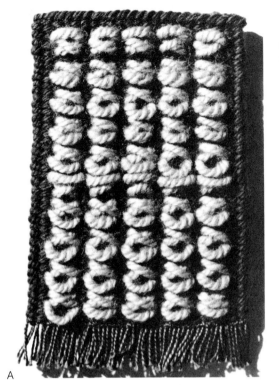

A

stitch, or another stitch that has a base of running stitch! This stitch is fun to play with and will provide accents or surface coverage.

Plush or Velvet Stitch

This charming old stitch has long held interest as a surface texture—a way to achieve a pile weave with a needle. The "naughts-and-crosses" effect (figure 3-39) is a bit unusual. With the loops kept quite low, it is satisfactory for a rug. The only very old references found on how to do this stitch showed the method shown in figure 3-40 (right). The extended length of the right-hand part of the loop is held down by a short diagonal stitch, so the effect is of a cross stitch above a loop. However, the loop is quite loose and movable. It is not very secure if cut ends are desired, although the directions suggest that it can be cut.

So another method was tried, the one shown in figure 3-40 (left), and this is more satisfactory where a precise, even surface is wanted. This version would be satisfactory for a join (figure 3-39). With each end of the loop sewn through

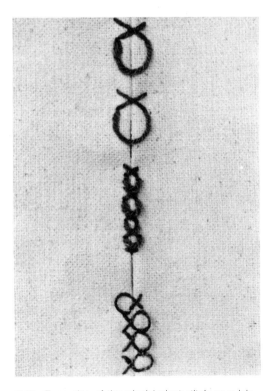

B

3-38. Top side (A), woven version, of the plush/ velvet stitch, showing the cross and loop. (B) Reverse side, cut pile and overshot; this two-faced pile weave uses surface texture for an effect.

3-39. Examples of the plush/velvet stitch as a join.

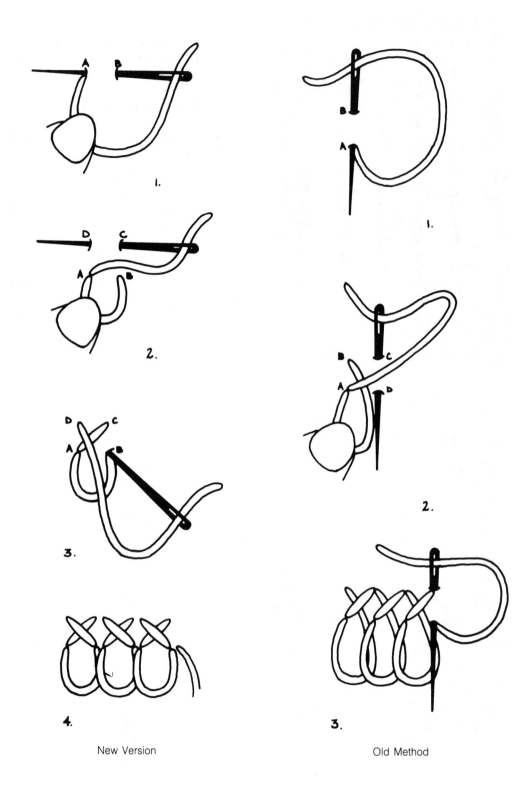

1.

2.

3.

4.

New Version

1.

2.

3.

Old Method

3-40. Plush or velvet stitch, two versions. On the right, the old version is shown, and on the left is my adaptation.

the cloth, it is more stable, but still has the cross and loop of the old method. It holds well if the loops are cut.

For a join, my method is to work from the bottom up, vertically, or from left to right, horizontally. The cross is the joiner and the loop helps to cover the seam.

Used as an edge stitch, several rows around a neckline will look like an attached collar (figure 3-14); make matching cuffs. An airy looped border can also be placed close to the edge so that the cross stitch is on the cloth and the loop hangs over the edge in a modest fringe. Or try working multiple rows of velvet stitch, one above the other, as a border for color-play. Rows spaced just far apart enough so the cross and loop both show, which is the distinctive feature of this versatile little stitch, is another possibility.

If you enjoy the challenge of adapting a stitch to a weaving method, try this one. Once under way, it goes fairly quickly. Use cut ends of weft. Weave one or two loops and crosses, take the weft out, and measure how much is needed for one unit of the stitch.

Weave several rows of ground weave. The method is just like the drawings for the embroidered version, except for the pause to weave the ground after the loop has been formed. Then, at the left, begin the first velvet stitch. Bring the surface weft up from the under side, leaving a short end on the back. Put the weft down between warps to the right for the width you want the loop. Take the weft end back and up to where the first end emerged, leaving a loop. Drop the end for now, and weave a few rows of ground weave. (If you are weaving a continuous row of stitches across the width, the first, or loop, part must be done all the way across before the rows of ground weave are woven and beaten in. Then the ends of each loop finish the cross part of the stitch over the woven ground.) Follow directions in figure 3-40, new version.

Thread weft end into a tapestry needle. Take it across from A to C, to the left and out at D. The second cross, from D to B, puts the end down between the warps. This cut end on the under side should be the same length as the first one. (Note the conformation of the weft yarns—two horizontal overshots and two cut ends in figure 3-38, B). Gently tug the first end down to the ground weave row; then the second weft placement is settled beside it. This ensures a smooth move into the cross, from the left tip of

the loop. Loops and crosses can be adjusted for tension and size after all is woven.

It might seem easier, if you want coverage in this stitch, to simply weave some inches, then go back and put the texture in with a needle. It was an interesting weaving exercise, and by weaving with cut ends, the bonus of the cut-pile surface texture on the reverse side was discovered. On a rug, the extra yarns on the back act as a cushion and the rug can be reversed.

Chevron Stitch

The chevron stitch joins, with edges apart or together. The slanting stitches must be drawn up to close the space. The straight stitches parallel the edges. It is a somewhat flexible join, but firm enough for garments, tablecloths, and other household weavings (figures 3-41 and 3-42).

Work from left to right (figure 3-43). Start with a straight stitch on the edge away from you, A–B. Come up below and at the center of that stitch, C. Slant down to the other edge and down at D. Go up at E and make another straight stitch to F. Slanting stitch G starts close to D, beginning stitch number two. Note that the straight stitches alternate on each edge and the slanted stitches always go from center to center of the straight stitches.

3-41. A close-up look at the chevron stitch. Also see figure 3-49.

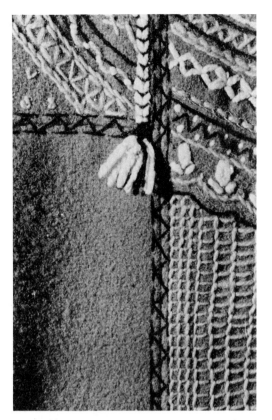

3-42. Chevron stitch as a butted seam on an embroidered vest.

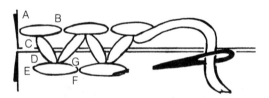

3-43. Chevron stitch. This can be a close join or open like a fagotting join.

Mountmellick Stitch

The Mountmellick stitch (figure 3-44) is a traditional white-work stitch from Ireland. Not seen as often as some others, it is well worth the learning. It is a surface stitch, historically, but a likely candidate for our group of joining stitches. It looks intricate, but falls into place if you follow the letters in the drawing (figure 3-45) and pay close attention to the needle positions. Practice it as a surface stitch with pearl 5 or stranded cotton floss to become familiar with it; then try it as a joining stitch.

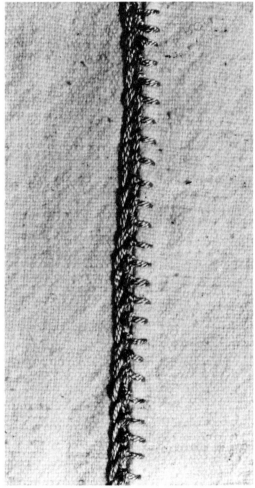

3-44. Detail of the Mountmellick stitch, on the African top, covering a stitched seam. It is also a firm join without the prestitching.

Work from the top down. Place the two edges together and bring the thread up from inside the hem. The two parts of the stitch that join are the first, A–B, slanting from edge to edge on the top, and B–C, a straight stitch underneath. Continuing, C goes up and over A–B. Then go down through A–C, with the thread under the needle, in a buttonhole stitch. Starting the next stitch, the slanting stitch from C–B is the same as A–B on the first stitch. In 5 on the drawing, note the arrow at C, where the buttonhole loop is started. Keep the raised look by pulling each stitch just into place, without tightening. In figure 3-44, the African tunic, stitch A–B was brought out quite far at the right. The looped part is all on the left section of cloth. The placement is a matter of choice and how the join is best made on your textile.

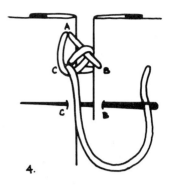

4.

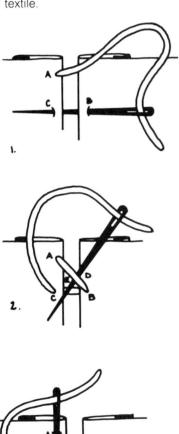

1.

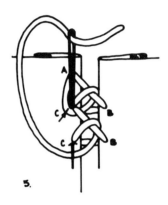

5.

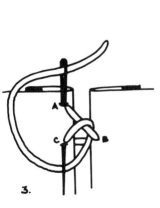

2.

3.

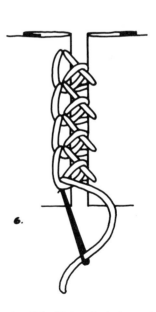

6.

3-45. Mountmellick stitch, adapted as a joining stitch.

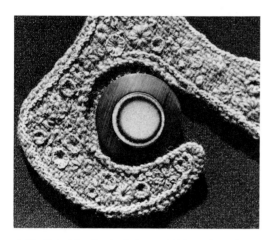

3-46. Palestrina knot stitch around the edge of a wool collar. It has a beadlike appearance in crisp linen thread.

Palestrina Knot

The Palestrina knot is another natural joiner because the stitch can be anchored on each side of the join. It is closely related to the Sorbello stitch. Work it vertically or horizontally. The teaching example on a hoop (figure 1-5) shows some of the many variations possible. It can curve, have no legs showing, or legs of different lengths. The size and fiber used make a definite change in the look of it. In a smooth-spun glossy linen thread (figure 3-46) along an edge, it is beadlike. In pearl 5 on the African tunic (figure 3-14), the stitch is more defined. The examples in the hoop are of wool worsted yarn and pearl cotton. Adapted as a joining stitch, it top-stitches a seam, with edges overlapping or just touching.

The drawing in figure 3-47 shows the Palestrina knot worked from left to right, horizontally. It can also be done vertically as a join (figure 1-4). The joining is at A–B and B–C, drawing the two edges together. The hitches are just like those on the Sorbello stitch. Coming from the center of the loop, the thread to D is the same as A–B and receives the hitches.

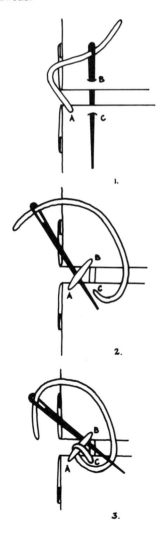

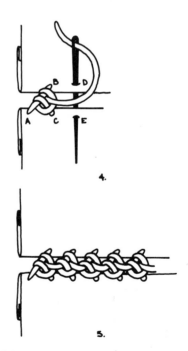

3-47. Palestrina knot stitch, adapted as a joining stitch. Work it straddling the seam line. Draw the edges close together or let the stitches center the space between. Also see figure 1-5 for variations, curved and straight.

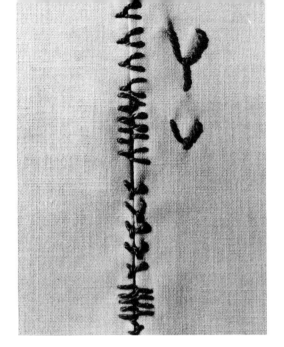

3-48. The Y stitch as a join. From the top: facing in one direction; alternating directions from side to side; slanting each stitch with leg on opposite side; close together, alternating direction; and very small, alternating. The two very large stitches show different lengths of the leg.

Y (or Fly) Stitch

The adaptable Y stitch has many applications for joining, edging, and surface uses. Figure 3-48 shows several ways to utilize this stitch for joining. It can be closely spaced to make a solid, firm line. It can be tall and slim or short and wide. This stitch is composed of a bar, caught with a straight vertical stitch in the center. Sometimes the long catch stitch version is called Y and the very short catch stitch a "fly" stitch. Tiny fly stitches cover an area with scattered stitches (powdering) as an alternative to the often-used seed stitch. Round flower shapes or snowflakes are created by facing the legs into the center or to the edge.

These variations are just a beginning. Work these stitches on top of each other or overlapping, in several colors and multistrands of thread. Figure 3-49 shows some different ways at the top. (The hoop also has examples of chevron and herringbone stitches.)

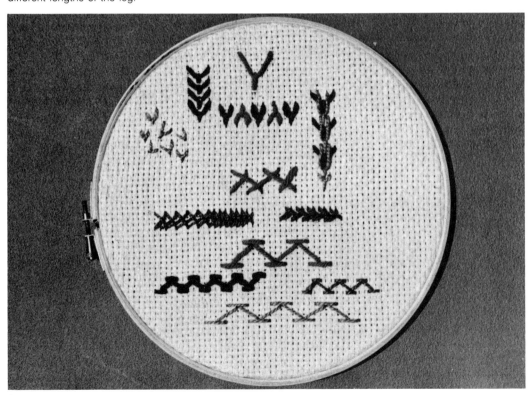

3-49. Examples of stitches and variations of each: (top) the Y stitch; (center) herringbone stitch, closed and open; (bottom) chevron stitch. All of these are good joiners.

Bar with Chain Joining Stitch

This joining stitch was a happening, not yet officially named, although it is similar to the raised chain band. The structure is a single chain stitch over the straight stitch that joins two edges. In figure 3-50 three bands are joined as an example of using this stitch to join lengths for an afghan or coverlet. The join is neat on the reverse side,

3-50. Three strips joined, with buttonhole stitch along the selvedges, then a bar with a chain stitch as a joining stitch. The warp-end finish is two rows of Philippine edge. This is a suggestion for an afghan or bedspread.

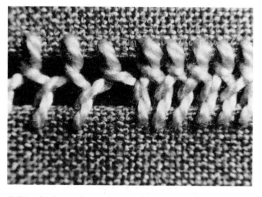

3-51. A close view of one of the many fagotting stitches. This one is far apart, then closer, and is used as a join.

so it is a good choice for a reversible textile. The join is flexible and the complete piece can be folded at the seams like an accordian. The selvedges to be joined are first sewn with an open buttonhole stitch (this can be worked on the loom). The joining stitch then slips through those stitches, not the cloth, so it is something like a lacing stitch.

To work this stitch, go under and up through the left-edge buttonhole stitch; then go over and down through the right-edge buttonhole stitch. Next, move up above the bar, and make one chain stitch over the bar; hold the yarn just below the bar to open the chain loop in order to center the stitch and help tighten it. Begin the second stitch by going under the buttonhole stitch on the left edge, and so on.

This stitch can be worked through the cloth at the edges instead of into buttonhole stitches. The warp end finish is two rows of Philippine edge, each worked from left to right.

Insertion and Fagotting Stitches

Insertion stitches are aptly named because they are stitches inserted between two edges, resulting in an open, lacy join. Most of the stitches shown in this chapter are suggested and shown as close joins, but they are also stitches that are used for insertion joins, in a more open way. The main characteristic of an insertion join is the use of fine threads and the open look. The stitches are anchored on each edge of the seam, then worked across, back and forth, firmly, but with some open space.

Fagotting is one of the insertion stitches. In figure 3-51, a simple fagotting stitch, open on the left and closed on the right, is shown. These open stitches are satisfactory where a bit of flexibility is needed in the seaming. Insertion stitches are very decorative and give a lightness to the work. They can make your joined seams the most important design element and focal point.

Insertion also refers to bands of lace or French insertion tapes woven in different widths and sewn between edges with embroidery stitches. It was very fashionable around the turn of the century. In 1908 my mother made her exquisite wedding dress all of lace insertion, tiny stitches, and fine lawn. Delicate fabrics and stitches are seen on fine handmade French lingerie and on baby clothing.

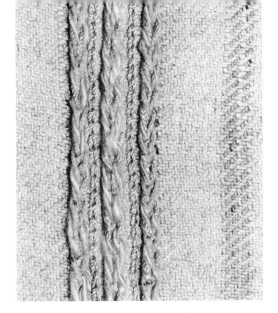

3-52. The five-strand joining on a silk bias-cut skirt. Three rows of the joining stitch, multiple strands of different spins of silk, are used with rows of chain stitch in between. The join flows with the graceful fall of the skirt, emphasizing the slant of the woven stripes. (Designer/weaver, Anita Mayer)

JOININGS
Five-strand Joining

The five-strand joining is fast and fun to do; it truly joins and can be made a feature of your project. Figure 3-52 shows a view of this joining on a bias-cut silk skirt. The design source for the skirt and a wide join was the Mexican indigo cotton skirts with wide stitched joins, which are made up so that the join slants across. Three rows of the five-strand stitch along with chain stitch rows sweep across the graceful rippling skirt, complementing the woven stripe.

To work this stitch (figure 3-53 and 3-54), place two edges close together and fasten them to a firm base. The only yarn that goes through the cloth and makes the join is number 1 in the drawing—the catch stitch. All of the other four are on the surface only. They can be bulky, lumpy, unspun, or multiple strands. Lay all four strands straight and in order. Leave some length at the top for later tasseling or other embellishment. Or, darn the ends in at the top or sew them in an embroidery stitch, drawing the edges together. The strands are moved in and out and are caught with the straight stitch after each move. Bring yarns 3 and 4 in to the center, catch down with 1, from a to b. Move them to the outside, bring 2 and 5 to the center, catch down, and so on. The drawing is for an expanded join; for a close one, the stitches would be much closer together.

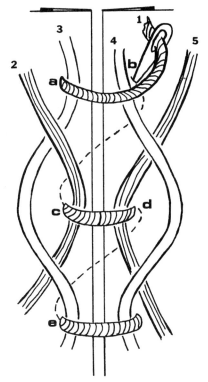

3-53. Five-strand joining. Strands are numbered in the drawing so the one catch stitch and four strands on the surface can be placed in succession. Only the catch stitch goes through the cloth, so the other yarns can be thick and textured.

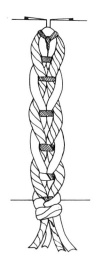

3-54. Completed five-strand joining.

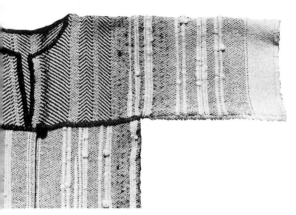

3-55. Change the color of seam-joining yarn on a rectangular jacket. The dark seam relates to and sets apart the yoke section. The light yarn minimizes the sleeve seam. This is a variation of the characteristic color changes in seams on Mexican and Guatemalan weavings. (Weaver, Robyn Jennings, Seattle, Washington)

Straight Stitch Join

A ribbed join results when a straight or satin stitch joins two pieces from edge to edge. Be careful not to pull the stitches up so tight that the material puckers, but just enough for a rounded ridge. A solid line of stitches closes the seam completely. Sometimes you may want to use an assortment of stitches, as in figure 3-56, for a more decorative seam. Several darker warps are at the selvedges for a contrasting stripe at the edges.

Bands as Joins and Extenders

The subject of bands is discussed in chapter 2, and much of that information applies when bands are used as a join. Sew a band to an edge, then line up the other edge, and sew the band on with a suitable stitch (figure 3-57). It is a great extender if more width or length is needed due to shrinkage, take-up, or a wrong measurement. Sew the selvedge edges of the band to the edge of the weaving.

For a style change, lengthen a sleeve or skirt by adding another material at the bottom; the band should be woven to correlate the colors and to act as a transition between the two materials. Or lengthen a dress or a skirt by adding a band at the waist. A sleeve seen often in early garments and costumes from many cultures is the drop shoulder, with or without a shoulder seam and with bands, either woven or embroidered, inserted around or up the sleeve. Put bands anywhere along the sleeve and shoulder.

3-56. Ribbed joins with satin (straight) stitches, plus a few others. Note the warp-end finishes also. At the left is Philippine edge with doubled ends; at right, the same technique with single ends.

3-57. A woven band covers the center seam on a linen tablecloth. The slanting band shows its use as an edge trim. (Weavers, Harold and Sylvia Tacker, Kirkland, Washington; photograph by Harold Tacker)

Bands will cover a seam and can be applied over an already-sewn seam as decoration. The seam will be reinforced by the addition. Sew carefully to avoid puckering. Be sure that band and textile have been preshrunk so that no unwanted crinkles appear later.

Tied Joins

This is another joining method that can be used with either side as the "right" side. You have a choice of knotted fringe or a line of knots only. The simple act of extending wefts beyond the selvedge provides ends for a tied joining. Or you may want to tie warp ends together. Tying can be snug and tight, close together, or loose and flexible. Double or triple knots secure the ties and provide the decorative line. Ends can be cut or loops. When cut ends are pushed to the inside, a textured seam is on the top. One precaution should be observed. After each extended weft row, the ground weave should return around the selvedge to confine it (figures 4-16 and 4-25). Otherwise, the long weft will cause the warps to drift out at the selvedge. Tying will prevent this, but it is a good idea to weave it this way so it is stable during the tying. The result will be smooth and better looking and will wear well. For a full fringe and close join, extend every other weft using double strands, or use two shuttles, alternating large and small yarns.

Pat Carr knitted a long, loose scarf of red wool with flecks of gray in the spin (figure 3-58). It grew to about eight feet, with knotted fringe added at each end. It was so long that she cut off a foot or so and made a jaunty cap of it. The ingenuity of fiber workers is boundless! Ends of the applied fringe are knotted together in double knots for a cascade of fringed trim. The extra width is caught together, creating a pouf at the top.

Two colors can be joined by tied weft loops in such a way that the loops lie on the opposite color. One or two overhand knots are made. With two knots, the ends have to be twisted so the colors fall on opposites, but the knot is tighter than with a single tie. Figure 3-59 shows a sampling for a rug.

Warp ends can be tied in the same way as the wefts, in which case plan to leave enough at each warp end for the ties. Figure 3-60 shows the method of making a pillow that is a square folded around a pillow form with ends tied. This is a small example (pincushion size) on two sampling bands. The two bands were joined with slip stitch to make a square, and the tied ends are warps. Weft ends could be woven on the other two sides so all seams are tied. Stuffing is put in, seams tied, then the selvedges joined with a needle stitch, plain or fancy. If the cut

3-58. Tied joining of the edges on a perky knitted cap. Cut ends are added as Ghiordes knot fringe. (Weaver/knitter, Pat Carr, Bainbridge Island, Washington)

3-59. Wefts woven out and back, leaving looped ends for a tied join.

ends are all inside, they add to the stuffing. When ends are out, it is a fringe trim.

A tied joining of warp or weft ends does not have to be straight and even with both edges meeting precisely. A wedge can be formed when the shoulder seam on a rectangular garment is made by tying ends (figure 3-61). The join will

3-60. A small example—pincushion size—of a pillow idea. These are warp-end ties. The ends are brought up and tied, then the selvedges are joined with stitches. The warp ends are pushed through to leave a row of knots, but the fringed side could be the outside, if preferred.

3-61. The tied join shapes a wedge for a shoulder seam. This shaping-joining idea would work for other places—for example, on a side join tapering out at the hem or hip.

be quite flexible and will follow the shoulder curve. When a shoulder seam is tied and shaped on a slant, there may be some slanting at the hem end; this can be accepted, or compensated for. On the other hand, the shoulder wedge shape can be quite slight, so hem-hang will not be a problem. A whole garment can be tied together at all seams, shaping where necessary by easing the width of the join. Tied gussets are flexible. A side seam can be tied with a gentle widening toward the bottom. There are many uses for this easiest of all joins, with no sewing necessary.

Coverlets, bedspreads, pillows as well as clothing can also be assembled with tied seams. Tie the warp ends of short lengths together for a long scarf or a shoulder band on a handbag. Tie small rug units together. Strips or units can be tied to make an afghan.

Weight or fasten the peices to be tied so they will be flat and straight. Pin the pieces to an ironing board or weight with a cloth-covered brick; or, for a small item, clamp them on a clipboard. Align the ends of each piece, and be very sure to pick ends up in order to ensure a smooth, ungathered join. Make an overhand knot or two. Tie so the edges just come together, or, if you are shaping the join, make a gradual slant. Try to tie each knot exactly in the center of the space and keep the tension even on each one. This method gives a knotted line on one side, fringed ends on the other.

Another method is to tie the first pair in a double knot which is then smoothed down into the space between sections; tie the second pair over the first one, smooth down, tie the third pair over, and so on, until the seam is closed and all ends are tied. The ends will be inside—out of sight—and the seam line will be a neat textured line. If the ends inside make an undesirable ridge, they can be clipped off at different lengths.

Ghiordes Knot Join

Another pile weave join, the Ghiordes knot (figure 3-62) beloved by rug weavers and seekers of high or low textures, also adapts itself to joining. All you need to work it is a pair of warps on the selvedge of two adjoining edges. Using a blunt tapestry needle, work from the bottom up. Cut the ends or loop them. For firmness and to avoid pulling, work the knots over more than one warp at each edge.

Embroiderers know this knot as "Turkey work" or needle rya stitch. Weavers know it as Ghiordes knot, rya or flossa knot, or Persian rug knot. The method is the same. Relationships and names of weaves and stitches are endlessly fascinating.

3-62. Ghiordes knot draws two selvedges together for a firm, shaggy needlework join. Take the joining thread under at the selvedge, at left, then up, over, and down through the opposite edge. Draw the stitch up close, and leave cut ends. Place the stitches one above the other, spaced as you wish.

Turkey work, the needle-made version of the Ghiordes or Smyrna knot, was done to imitate woven Turkish carpets. Berlin work was an imitation of Turkey work, which was an imitation.

Crochet Joins

Crochet is a highly satisfactory technique that combines easily with handwoven textiles. It is almost a universal choice among weavers for joins and edges in clothing and household weavings. Each application is different, and there is plenty of room for innovative designing. Color is one area of the designing that varies the appearance. Whether the basic edge stitch is worked right into the cloth or into a needle-stitched edge is another variable. The size hook, tension, kind of yarn, width of join, and number of rows all play a part in the variations. In figure 3-63 a beautifully even, controlled crochet join and edge on a pearl cotton tunic is shown. The white line in contrast to the woven stripe and matching edge crochet sparks it up.

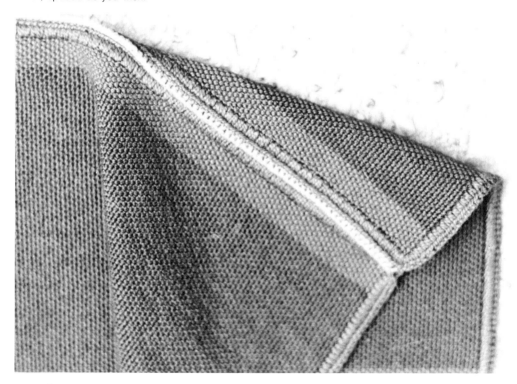

3-63. Continuous lines of even crochet on the shoulder and drop sleeve of a slipover tunic. (By Jean Sullivan)

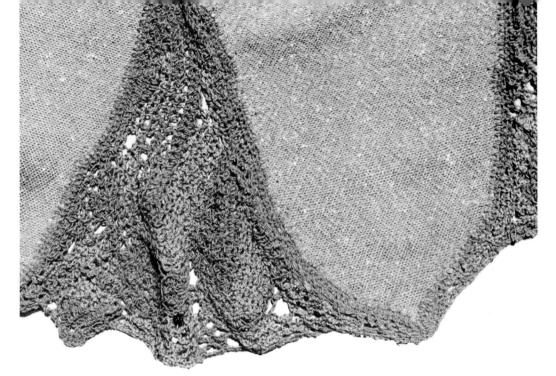

3-64. A lacelike crocheted gusset in a bias-cut, finely woven circular skirt. The gusset is freely crocheted, so it folds and flares. The edge of the skirt has crochet continuing to the next triangular gusset. This is a casual but planned effect. (Designer/weaver, Robyn Jennings, Seattle, Washington)

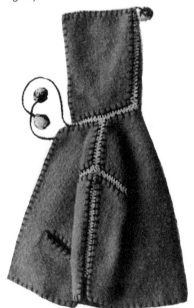

3-65. Side view of a child's jacket made in Greece. This bright little garment has a number of good design ideas. Crochet joins the hood to the jacket, continuing the shoulder join. (Courtesy, Susan Snover, Seattle, Washington)

A triangular gusset shapes a skirt or flares a decorative weaving and acts as a joining element. Flare a cuff by weaving slits then crocheting insets. Some African shirts are made with long slim triangles inserted all the way around for a widening at the hemline. Anita Mayer borrowed that idea for a long sleeveless gown with narrow gussets crocheted in. Subtle shading of colors, with dark at the hemline lightening toward the waist, gave a slimming effect.

The details and construction of the child's jacket (figure 3-65) can be translated into an adult-size coat or jacket. The cloth is a napped blanket material, dense but soft, in a rich green. The edge stitch is large blanket stitch in black wool yarn. All of the seams are joined with bright red yarn, crocheted back and forth through the blanket-stitched edges. Slits are left at the wrist and at each side seam. Slanting slit pockets are also edged with the blanket stitch. The jacket is lined with black before the edge stitching is done, so the stitches go through both layers. Edge-stitching through the lining is a good idea to keep the lining in place. The line of joining from wrist up the sleeve and shoulder, around the back of the neckline, and to the hood is good design with the unbroken line. The shoulder seam is slanted for a good fit. Perky crocheted cords with fat, round pom-poms in two colors tie at the neck and crown the tip of the hood.

C-1. Tie-dyed shawl from Gugerat, India, lined with printed silk. It has elaborate embellishment of shisha (mirror) embroidery and other stitches, weft tassels, and ends finished with miniature tassels crowded together. (From the collection of Leslie Grace, Folk Art Gallery, La Tienda, Seattle, Washington)

C-2. Camel saddlebag from Pakistan. This is a study of edge and joining stitches, tassels and cords, and color and design. (Courtesy, Dina Barzel, Bellevue, Washington)

C-3. Horsehair tassels (dyed) with netted crowns, on a finger-woven band. This is part of camel gear. (From the collection of Leslie Grace)

C-4. A long length of black cotton, with ends embellished with fine chain stitch stripes, red binding, and charming little discs. The decoration is on each corner of each end. The small wheels are covered in red cotton, then embroidered in segments of color. (From Laos, by a Tai woman, author's collection)

C-5. *Roan Landscape,* a fine example of a visual join, carrying the design along in separate sections. It is tapestry on a crackle weave threading, design laid in. (Designer/weaver, Nancy Lyon, Concord, New Hampshire; photograph by Nancy Lyon)

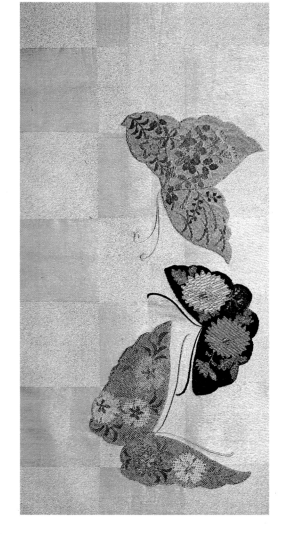

C-6. Obi woven of silk and gold, enhanced with three exquisite butterflies in Rozashi technique, needleworked on fine silk mesh, then applied to the obi. Rozashi is an extremely fine stitch, usually found on museum-quality pieces. It has been recently "discovered" and studied in this country. (Author's collection)

C-7. *Southwest Choir* illustrates the use of surroundings, or edges, around a small tapestry. It is mounted on hand-loomed Belgian linen stretched over a canvas covered frame. (By the author)

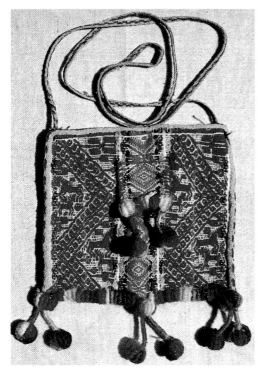

C-9. Coca bag from Tarebuco, Bolivia, with the wrapped edge and pom-poms shown in figures 4-33 and 4-44. (Collection of Leslie Grace)

C-8. *Jimbaori,* a garment beautifully embellished on the back with an embroidered butterfly. (Designer/weaver, Anita Mayer)

C-10. A tote bag inspired by the small coca bags and wrapped pom-poms. (Designer/weaver, Polly Matsumoto, Florida)

C-11. Example of an edge woven on while the main weaving is being woven. It is of wool, with plain weave and Greek soumak triangles. At the top is a variation in laid-in yellow pearl.

C-12. Luxurious jewel-toned velvets and silks make the back (and front) panels of a purple velvet caftan. A variety of embroidery stitches join the pieces. (Artist, Paul Albiston, Seattle, Washington; photograph by Pat Albiston)

Patchwork

Patchwork, or piecing, is just a matter of joining piece to piece to piece, until the size and shape required is reached. Romantic, traditional "crazy quilts" of silk, satin, and velvet patches were usually hand-stitched and then every known embroidery stitch embellished and outlined the rich pieces. A fond childhood memory is sleeping under one and competing with my sister to choose the most beautiful patch and then make up stories about the ladies who wore the elegant gowns and hats fashioned from the lovely fabrics.

Pat Albiston made a velvet patchwork caftan from new cloth, a reversal of my fantasies about gowns into patches! Figure 3-67 shows how she constructed it, and C-12 the lovely result. Traditional patchwork is pieces sewn together. The variation here is that shaped pieces are basted on an interfacing (which becomes the lining), edges just touching; then embroidery stitches are worked over the cut edges, completely covering them.

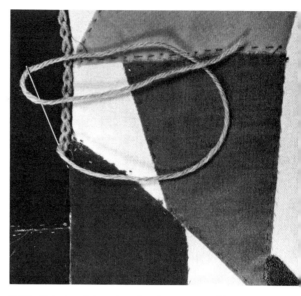

3-67. Velvet patchwork caftan in progress. The finished caftan is shown in C-12. (Artist, Pat Albiston, Seattle, Washington; photograph by Beverly Rush)

3-66. Black suede leather and black yarns are used for this handsome coat, but it is far from dull! The combination of fine, smooth black wool, a silky textured wool, and mohair yarn that catches highlights, and the velvety suede leather make it rich and elegant. It is joined and edged with crochet of a fine black wool yarn. A nice design element occurs where suede joins wool. The perforations in the leather add a line of dots which makes the join look like hemstitching. (Weaver, Jean Sullivan)

Another patchwork method, on knitted fabric, is shown in figures 3-68 and 3-69. The cut pieces are basted to muslin, with spaces between, then joined with Italian insertion stitch. The basting stitches are removed after completion. Only the beginning and ending of the joining stitches go through the muslin, with ends left unknotted, so the muslin can be pulled away when all of the joinings are complete. The ends of yarn are secured, and the unlined blouse is finished.

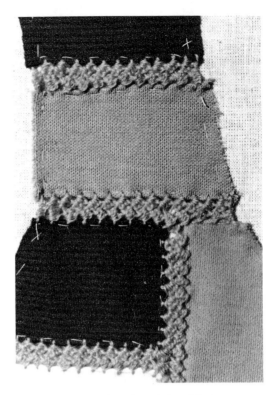

3-69. Wide Italian insertion stitches join the cut pieces. (Artist, Jill Nordfors, Gig Harbor, Washington; photograph by Beverly Rush)

3-68. Patchwork of knitted fabric for an overblouse, ready to complete with joining stitches.

Arrowhead Tack

A practical stitch with a practical use, the arrowhead tack (figure 3-70) can be a decorative accent, too. Work an arrowhead at the end of a seam, at the peak of a pleat or to finish off tucks. Place it wherever there is a weak area that may easily come unsewn or tear, such as on a shoulder seam at the neckline or on the V at the neck. It reinforces and decorates. When worked in a matching color, it does not conflict with other trims. The arrowhead tack is seen on finely tailored skirts, such as the perennially classic camel hair skirts with hand-worked details. On a vintage coat, fine tucks at the shoulders can be finished with small black arrowheads. The tack performs a necessary function on a handwoven poncho at the seam junctures to keep the seams from stretching or loosening when slipping on and off over the head. Anita Mayer works the tacks inside of a garment at stress points. In a contrasting color, arrows will act as a small trim. The example in figure 3-71

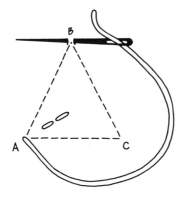

also has a hand-picked seam; they go together in fine finishing and are hallmarks of fine, complete craftsmanship.

Preparing an edge, either on the loom or on the textile, leads to joining, which leads to enrichment, thence to embellishment, to closures, and so on—until you have worked through a complete handcraft experience. Now—on to the next chapter, for trims and embellishments!

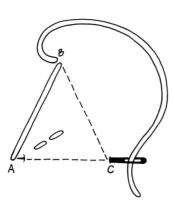

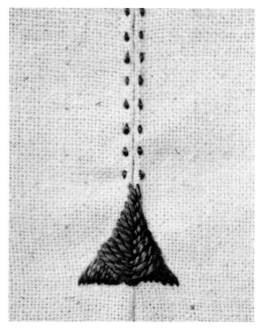

3-71. Arrowhead tack at the top of a pleat. The seam is hand-picked (tiny, evenly spaced running stitches). On a wool skirt or coat, it would probably be worked in a matching thread.

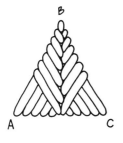

3-70. Arrowhead tack. (Drawing by Beth Workman)

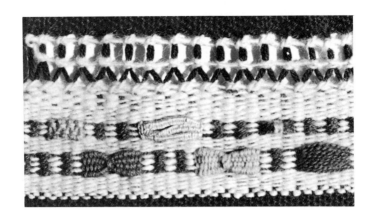

4. Trims, Fringes, Tassels, and Embellishments

When a garment or other basic weaving is planned and carefully made, your reward is the fun of embellishing and trimming. This is where your individual style, imagination, and skills have free play. Enhance a tunic with rich embroidery; make dozens of tassels to trim a holiday tree or the edge of a wallpiece. This chapter offers ideas and methods for fabricating or weaving-in a variety of trims. Some are fanciful—many are practical. They will help to add another dimension to your designing and weaving.

The word *trims* was chosen to be part of the overall title of this book because it encompasses so many of the techniques and methods presented. Definitions of trim include such words as embellish, ornament, adorn, and decorate. Other definitions apply, too: neat, tidy, in good order, appropriate, in the right place, properly prepared, and in balance.

Some procedures used to fabricate weavings produce trims, so in the sections on edges and

4-1. A stunning brass and silk ornament from Tibet, to be worn as jewelry at neckline or waist. It qualifies as a trim, a tassel, and an added embellishment. (From the collection of Anita Mayer, Anacortes, Washington)

ends you will find examples of trims resulting from the finishing. Fringes, tassels, and other embellishments are detailed in this chapter. These techniques and methods are separated into those done on the loom or as part of a complete trim; and those that are finished or fabricated off from the loom and applied. Some are fabricated and added as an accessory, not necessarily attached—an addition.

4-2. Fringed band sewn to the edge of a bedspread. It is a trim as well as a reinforcement. (Weaver, Sylvia Tacker; photograph by Kent Kammerer)

TRIMS

A trim can be a row of embroidery stitches or a small woven pattern on an edge; it can be a band woven in blending colors sewn to a bed-spread edge (Figure 4-2) or a flamboyant grouping of tassels, beads, and fringes along the end of a wallhanging, such as the one shown in figure 4-3. Try whatever suits your fancy and the product you are creating. The many ideas, methods, and techniques for trims are grouped in a semblance of order, although it is sometimes difficult to decide what is a trim and what is an embellishment. Look through this chapter and the others to find what is right—plain or ornate—for an edge, an end, or other locations.

4-3. Tassels with beaded crowns, assorted wooden beads, and wrapped rings crowd the bottom edge of a wallhanging. (Artist, Sue Roach, Portland, Oregon; photograph by Beverly Rush)

4-4. Knitted cords and knitting needles. A tiny, plump pincushion edged with a fine commercial cord, coiled around at one corner, is an idea for a pillow with a knitted cord edging.

The Knitted Cord

Intrigued and fascinated by the knitted cord—both the doing and the myriad ways to use it—I have elevated it not to a work of art, certainly, but to a few notches above mitten strings! The adaptable, unassuming little knitted cords are used throughout this book as edges, trimmings, lacing, bindings, or parts of a closure, so refer to the other uses as well as to those detailed here.

The knitted cord is so simple to do—it is well-named the "idiot's delight"—but, as with many simple crafts, it is all in what use you make of it and how you design with it. Knitted cords of different yarns and spins and colors fill various needs and are very compatible with handwovens.

In figure 4-4 an assortment of knitted cords and needle sizes shows some possibilities. Using every size of double-end aluminum needle, all kinds of yarn were tried: heavy rug yarns, handspun wools and silk, pearl cottons, fine and coarse wools, textured and smooth, and metallic threads on a core. Knitting cords is quite therapeutic! It is a good change of pace from weaving and stitching and is almost a mindless occupation, soothing and repetitious. Yards of cord can be turned out while you play a waiting

game—flying across the country, in a traffic tie-up, waiting for an appointment or your child's ballet lesson. Carry a small ball of yarn and a pair of knitting needles with you. Before you know it, you will have some very interesting lengths of cord to use and perhaps save yourself some stress!

You probably made cords like this on a spool when you were a youngster. You are knitting a tube. The size varies with the number of stitches cast on and the size of the yarn and needles. My experiments took me from the finest single-ply wool on the smallest double-end needles, through all sizes of needles and yarn, up to large rug wool on the largest needles. Uneven spins, smooth yarns, and thick and thin handspuns are in the examples shown. Handspun silk cords are soft and luxurious. Rug yarn makes stiff, coarse cords. Each trial suggests a different use:

- Need a belt or sash to match your handwoven dress? Knit several from the same yarn. Wear three at once, tied, with tasselled ends.
- Need a trim or a collar? Knit some cords in colors. Fasten rows of them together with slides or beads (figure 4-5).
- Couch rows around the neck and wrist with embroidery stitches.

- Need a lacing length? Knit it and knot, tassel, or bead the ends.
- Need gimp or binding for a cushion or a chair? See the example in figure 2-22.
- Bind all around the edge of a jacket or sweater with knitted cord, over the edge, or along the top edge. Knit it so that the tube is not pulled into a full round (figure 2-21).
- Knit a handbag handle. So the handle won't be too stretchy, use a firmly spun yarn and tight stitches. Remember this is a hollow tube, and, if your yarn is too elastic, a length of strong twine can be run through it.
- A textured heavy length can be couched on an edge, with stitches widely spaced.
- Coil cords into coasters, seat pads, or small rugs.
- Yards and yards will be needed, but try some for weft as accent rows.
- Lengths of fine cord sewn on an edge in continuous loops make buttonholes.
- Coil and sew cords into buttons, medallions, or frogs.
- Take one or more turns of the cord around the collar of a tassel and use cord for a hanger.
- Couch cords to cover a seam and reinforce a join.
- Braid three knitted cords for a three-dimensional accent.

Double-pointed knitting needles are a necessity, because you will knit from each end, alternately. When casting on the stitches, leave a few inches of yarn to close the end. Keep the stitches relaxed enough so they slide easily, but tight enough to make a smooth closed tube. Aluminum needles are very slippery, so be careful not to let the cord slide off. All is not lost, however, if they do slip off and you lose a few rows in the blink of an eye. Just pick up the stitches, being careful to slip the needle into them so they face in the right direction. You can check on which end of the needle to use so the top side of the cord is up and to your right, with the working yarn coming up from the bottom stitch. This crossing over from bottom to top is what creates the closed tube as the yarn is drawn up by the pull on the cord after each stitch.

Cast on three or more stitches (refer to figure 4-4). The number of stitches is determined by the size of the cord wanted. Be sure the yarn always comes from the bottom stitch up to the knitting end. The sequence of a complete row

is: knit all of the stitches; tug down on the tail, at the same time pulling up on the yarn over your finger, to tighten up the last stitch; slide stitches to the opposite end of the needle; turn the needle so the cord is again toward you, top up, and the yarn is feeding from the bottom stitch; and knit all of the stitches. Continue the knit, slide, turn sequence until the length of cord is what you need. After a few rows, you will see the tube forming as the rows draw together.

A flat cord, slightly open at the back, can be made when the working yarn is not pulled up quite as snugly as for the closed tube. This cord is a perfect edge binding, with the cord placed over the edge (figure 2-21). It can be sewn on invisibly or with an embroidery stitch. It also works as a flat edge binding on just the top side of the selvedge or hem.

4-5. Inspired by the Masai beaded dance necklaces, a neckpiece was assembled from knitted cords of silk and wool yarns in warm colors. Yarn tails were left at the end of each cord; these were threaded through the rosewood flat slide. The ends are tasselled. The neckpiece is flexible and sized so it slips over the head, eliminating any need for a working fastener.

4-6. Long warp ends at the bottom of the scroll. One row of Greek soumak was used in the last row of weaving. The wrapping is the system of wrap-knot-wrap-knot, tight and secure.

4-7. Warp ends of each stripe are braided and folded to the outside edge of a handbag.

FRINGES

Fringes are a natural happening. When warp ends are unwoven, you have a fringe! If you do not want it, hem the edge. To keep the textile from becoming unwoven, some sewing or knotting is required. If the warp ends tangle, they can be braided, wrapped, or otherwise protected. So there you are—well on the way to some creative fringing and edge enhancement. If the edge does not have an integral fringe, one can be added in a number of different ways..

Fringes are swingy and bold, demure and subtle, bright and ornamental. Like tassels, they can have significance relating to rank and occasion (for example, fringed epaulets on uniforms). They add movement and excitement. The surrey with the fringe on top was more glamorous than one with a sober plain edge! Fringes dance on costumes and umbrellas. In Victorian times, just about everything was fringe-trimmed, from fireplace mantels to prams, to gowns, to bead-fringed lampshades. Maori and Hawaiian skirts are fringed waistbands. Northwest Indian cedar-bark capes and Chilkat blankets have deep fringe. Beautifully crafted leather Indian costumes bear fringed edges of cut leather.

Fringes are in our past and present. There are countless variations and methods of making them. Only a few of the many can be presented here—some familiar methods and perhaps some you have not seen. Use yarns, threads, beads and feathers; your own projects and observations will suggest modes and other materials.

The repetitious but necessary admonition, plan ahead, is of prime importance here if you intend to use the warp or weft as fringe; you must be sure to select the right yarn and color and to see that special work is done at the proper time.

Integral Fringes

Long warp ends at the bottom of the scroll are an example (figure 4-6). The warp ends are grouped and held with one row of Greek soumak. It not only separates the bundles, but keeps the weft from moving down. It is a good practice to make a row such as this before braiding or working other finishes on the warps. It defines the edge and is good protection for the weaving. After being cut from the loom, the ends are caught together then separated out. A band of wrapping, each row knotted, gathers all the ends. Next, a very short braid of all ends then three groups of ends are wrapped and knotted. Finally each group is wrapped again near the end. See Tassels for wrapping methods.

The following examples are of quite simple ways to treat warp-end fringe, where the warp has been chosen well and is of interesting yarns. A rather simple and obvious treatment of warp ends at the top edge of a handbag is shown in figure 4-7. The warps are braided to echo the stripes in the bag. The handle is a firm braid in the same yarns, ending with tassels and sewn at the top corners. The striped warps in a band shown in figure 4-8 are separated out so each stripe is braided. The braided ends are crossed, making a lattice pattern, and are caught with a wrapping. The ends are wrapped and cut into short fringe. A mixed warp of off-white wool and textured silk (figure 4-9) is divided into bundles which are braided then wrapped, with long ends left as fringe. The edge is first worked back and forth in three rows of Czech edge (figure 2-42), then the material is turned over and one row is worked on the reverse side. This makes a line of knots on the back so both sides are neat looking. Note the deep shadow line where the three rows form a rounded edge. Silk warp is divided and knotted then crossed and knotted again, with very long ends, in the example shown in figure 4-10.

4-9. Rows of Czech edge create a shadow line above the braided warps. White wools and textured silk are used.

4-8. Warp ends braided and crossed with short wrapped ends. Warps are grouped by color.

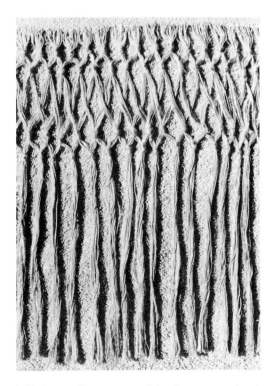

4-10. Long silk warps on a tabard are crossed and knotted. (Weaver, Joan Walker, Renton, Washington)

4-11. Twisted, wrapped, and knotted warp ends on narrow bands.

Twisted Warp Ends

Twisting warp ends is a classic method found in many cultures, particularly on Scandinavian weavings. It is simple, effective, and easy to do. Figure 4-11 is a good example. First a row of Philippine edge was worked, then the warp ends were twisted in groups of four; the two inside groups were tightly wrapped first, before twisting, for a variation. An overhand knot finishes the end.

Figure 4-12 shows a sampling of twisted warp ends, using different numbers of warp—from four to about fourteen. About six inches of two-thread monks cloth was unwoven, leaving fine thread warps on which to experiment. Do this on a handwoven scrap with long warp ends, or ravel out to get the ends. Note that knots and wrapping are at the top of some. When you have not been able to weave-in a knotted row, a single overhand knot provides a stabilizing start for fringe on an already-woven textile.

Before twisting or otherwise finishing warp-end fringe, work at least one row of a Czech, Philippine, Greek soumak or one of the similar weft safeguarding edges detailed in chapter 2. By doing this, the heading will have more definition than if the twists were to be begun directly under the last woven row. Divide the warp ends evenly, putting two or more strands in each group. The number will be determined by the size twist you want, how the fringe is to be spaced, and size and sett of the warp. Keep a firm hold on

the strands involved until the final set or the twist gets away from you. Twist first one then the other group in the same direction. Put the two twists together, and twist them in the opposite direction. Over-twist each time, until the yarn curls and kinks. Before you let go, knot all the ends in an overhand knot (or a hitch with just one of the strands) to secure the ends and save the twists.

Other manipulation or additions can be done once the twists are held in place. The strands will loosen a bit. Some yarns hold the twist better than others. This happened with yarn spun from one of our big old rams. It was as tough as he was—so those ends were knotted, one overhand knot after the other. If you find your yarn stubbornly loosens, then accept the characteristics of that yarn and let it hang untwisted and wrap or braid it! If the group includes too many ends and is worked too tight and close to the weaving, it will pucker the edge. Try to keep the edge flat and smooth for the best effect. The suggested row of warp finish before the twisting will help to keep the weaving flat. If twisted fringe is what you absolutely *must* have, even when confronted by yarn with a mind of its own, it might help to set the twist by very light steaming from a steam iron or teakettle—without touching the yarn.

4-12. Sampling twisted warp ends with various numbers of fine warp groups, on two-thread monks cloth. Notice the different amounts of take-up in the lengths; they were all even to start.

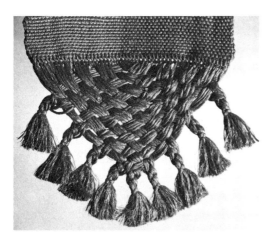

4-13. Woven warp ends. Several strands of binder-twine were woven in groups then braided and tasselled. (Weaver, Hope Munn, Mercer Island, Washington; photograph by Kent Kammerer)

4-14. Warp ends knotted on themselves with overhand knots, then half of each group knotted across.

Other Twisted Fringes

On integral fringe or on fringe made separately in strips, beads can be added. An especially opulant effect is achieved by slipping a tiny glass bead on a fine warp end and taking the cut end back up to be fastened into the edge. The bead is left at the bottom, the strands twisted above it. Beaded fringes, crowded and rippling, are seen on colorful textiles from Afghanistan. Sometimes two or three of the small beads are strung at the end of the twisted fringe. This method of twisting one (or a small group) very long warp end and weaving or knotting the cut end up into the edge is an excellent way of preventing ravelled cut warps, especially if the yarn is loosely spun or plied. Tassels are made this way, also, just doubling the ends back and catching them into the tassel top (see the tassels on the Pakistan camel bag, C-2.).

Woven Warp Ends

This is a variation of woven warp-end fringe. Hope Munn wove the coarse binder-twine ends shown in figure 4-13 loosely, then finished them with a short braid and knotted wrap. This fiber is very stiff and slippery, so it was a very good example of letting the material have its own way. The ends are combed, unplying the fiber.

Knotted Warp Ends

A striped band with a very short fringe is shown in figure 4-14. Each bundle is separated into two, then knotted on itself with a succession of overhand knots (figure 4-15). Each group is then knotted to the next one. The effect is of a row of openwork followed by full short ends. This treatment, simple and fast, rewards you with a slightly different, casual texture. It can be used on almost any weaving but would be especially nice on rugs as a change from the usual hanging fringes, and it is short enough not to be a heel-catcher.

4-15. Overhand knot.

Fringe All Around

This can be done on the loom for fringe on all edges (figure 4-16). Choose a warp that is suitable for fringe at top and bottom ends. Weave a weft fringe with a skeleton warp tied at each edge to gauge the loop lengths. Note that the weft is taken around the selvedge between the loop ends to contain the selvedge warp. This example has nothing more done to either ends or edges. If it was to be used just as woven, a row of Greek soumak should have been woven at each end to safeguard the weft.

A small-size example—a thumbnail sketch for a rug—was used to try out various techniques and fringe ideas (figure 4-17). The bottom edge is a close row of Ghiordes knots. The fringe along each side is woven in with lark's-head hitches (figure 4-18) on the selvedge warps. The body of the rug is in Greek soumak, and the fringe is added at the sides as required for fullness—about one lark's head to two or three rows of soumak. The last row at the top edge is woven in Ghiordes knots, completing the frame of fringe. This method of fringing all around applies to edging mats, scarves, bedspreads, or rugs of any size.

4-17. A sampling for a rug. Fringe is on all sides; lark's-head knots are at the sides, around selvedge warps; and Ghiordes knots are at top (facing up) and bottom. All were woven row by row. The pattern is in Greek soumak.

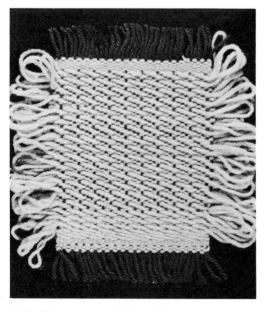

4-16. Fringe all around. The dark cut ends are warp. The looped fringe is weft. (Photograph by Kent Kammerer)

4-18. Lark's-head hitch. Cut the weft a bit more than twice the length you want for the finished end. Fold the weft over so ends are even. Put the loop under the warp and pull the ends through the loop, snugging it up. When you want the ends sideways, as in figure 4-17, put the loop under the left selvedge warp and pull ends to face the left. For the right-facing ends, put the loop under the right selvedge warp and pull ends to the right.

Weft Fringe on a Band

A fringe-end and selvedge (figure 4-19) finish, with weft fringe and warp ends on a narrow band, could be on a belt, collar, or a decorative household weaving. At the end of a narrow warp, lay in large yarn or bundles of weft with ends several inches long, in each shed, beat, change shed, and beat to press the yarn in for a rounded look. Continue, with a few rows woven between the thick inserts, as many times as desired. The warp shows as it passes over the heavy weft groups, so be sure to choose an attractive one. The weft ends show only at the edges. The exaggeration and the thickness of the large amount of weft is an unexpected finish on a finely woven narrow band. It is a nice change from warp ends and tassels. Ribbed rows with thick weft fringes can also be woven in wide widths, laying the thick weft bundles in. Try this on bedspreads or wall pieces.

4-19 Weft fringe in bundles, on a narrow band. Weave thick wefts on wider widths, also.

Layered Fringe

When weaving layered fringe, start with the warp ends as the first layer. Weave a row of Greek soumak, either leaving the warps straight or drawing them into groups. Weave several rows, then add a row of Ghiordes knot, cut or looped, overlapping the warp ends slightly. Weave a few more rows, then another row of fringe. Each row of fringe can be a different color, or colors might change within each row. A whole spectrum of color-play is possible, limited only by your own good taste and the suitability to the use of the weaving. Plain-woven rows may show between the rows of fringe. With fine yarns, three rows plus the warp ends will give elegance and physical weight to the hem of a long skirt. A deep, lush border of many fringe rows might enrich a luxurious bedspread. Take this idea almost *too* far and add some tassels! Rows of fringe can be woven as bands, then sewn on wherever wanted.

Applied Fringe

The natural and logical termination of a warp is a fringe. But often a fringe is the perfect embellishment, fabricated off the loom and added to enhance an edge or surface. The common denominator of all trims and enrichments is their truly endless scope. Ask a dozen fiber artisans for an applied fringe and you will get a dozen varieties. Some applied fringes are woven as strips to be sewn on; some are hitched on in yarn groups; others are fashioned as tassels but applied as fringes; or woven cloth is raveled for a binding-fringe (figure 4-26). Those presented here are just hints of the exciting world of fringe.

Fastfringe

Fastfringe, so named because it *is* fast, is a quick and easy way to fabricate yards and yards of fringe without having to prepare lengths of warp or weft (figure 4-20). It is wound directly from the spool or skein onto a gauge.

4-20. Fastfringe, three stages: (top) on a cardboard gauge and chain stitch; (middle) off from the gauge; (bottom) sewn to an edge.

Continuous fastfringe can be made to any length. Use cardboard (or a block of wood) as a gauge for the width of the fringe; cut a slit near each end in order to hold the yarn at the start and finish; or tape the end to the gauge (the ends will be sewn in when placing the fringe on the cloth). The example in figure 4-20 is of wool knitting worsted, but any fiber or spin can be used. The yarn should be wound loosely enough to be slipped off easily, but keep an even tension. Place yarns so they just touch.

When the gauge is full, hand-sew one row of chain stitch over two or more warps at a time on the top side of the gauge only. Chain with needle or crochet hook. Leave a tail end to help anchor the fringe to the cloth and to secure the chain.

When complete, slip the fringe off the gauge and continue winding another gauge-full, chain, and so on, until the continuous length needed is finished. Figure 4-20 shows three stages of the process: on the cardboard and the stitching; off the gauge; and sewn to an edge with added stitches above and below the chain. To attach the fringe, flatten the coil of fringe so the chained row is at the top, or at the center, or where you will. Lay the cloth on a table and pin the fringe on. Sew with a hand-stitch (a running stitch through the chains is the simplest). After the first sewing, any number of rows and stitches and colors can be added to widen and embellish. An elaborate heading can be embroidered on the fringe. You can flatten the fringe and sew it on with rows of stitches in the center, the fringe loops at each side. Apply fringe rows, or make small sections and apply them as medallions here and there as accents. The colors used and the various stitches chosen will give totally different effects.

Figure 4-21 shows a richly full application in silk on a handwoven silk and cottolin top by Anita Mayer. The natural silk fastfringe is sewn on with several rows of chainstitch in two colors. The ends are cut. Groups of ends are knotted, just under the stitched rows, in overhand knots. The ends are so closely set that the groups hang full. Note how the length of the fringe sewn on the selvedge edge of the rectangle tunic creates little cap sleeves. There is also a subtle row of hand-stitching in matching silk thread around the neckline.

4-21. A slipover top with silk fastfringe sewn on with rows of chain stitches. (Weaver, Anita Mayer)

Weave Two Strips of Weft Fringe at Once

Set up two separate narrow warps the width you want the heading. The space between is the length of the fringe for each piece (for a fringe three inches long, the space between will be six inches). Weave across each warp with one weft. Unwoven weft stretches between the two warp groups. The selvedges become the tops, or the headings. It is necessary to take the weft around the selvedges every other pick to keep the warps from floating. Cut the wefts down the center, and you have two strips of cut fringe (figure 4-22).

Doubled Warp Fringe

One way of making an integral warp fringe is shown in figures 4-23, in progress on the loom, and in 4-24, folded up with the two headings hemmed together. The fringe is of full, looped warps. In this example, the heavy wool yarn twisted itself into groups when it was cut from the loom, making an interesting twisted fringe.

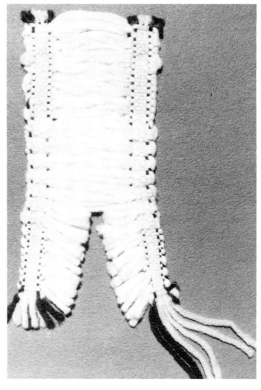

4-22. Weave two strips of fringe at once. Weave the weft across, making two headings, then cut up the center for separate strips after removal from the loom.

Body of the Textile

Second Heading
Greek Soumak Row

Unwoven Warp
(The Fringe)

Greek Soumak Row
First Heading

4-23. Double, uncut warp fringe woven on the loom. Later, the heading is brought up and hemmed to the body of the weaving. The unwoven warps become looped fringe.

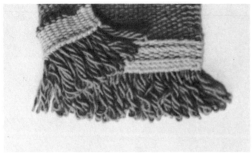

4-24. Doubled warp fringe. The plain-weave heading is sewn along the back of the top side patterned heading. The warps are folded back, making them doubled. In the coarse wool yarn of this sample, they twisted by themselves.

Weave an inch or more like a heading, with the last row Greek soumak. Leave unwoven warp for several inches, twice the length you want the finished fringe to be. Above the unwoven warp, weave another heading the same size as the first one, with Greek soumak as the first row. This will be the top-side hem. This completes the weaving for the fringe. Continue, weaving the body of the textile—coverlet, skirt, scarf, or rug. If you want this same fringed edge at the other end, repeat the above, in reverse order. Cut from the loom and fold the first heading up to cover the back of the second heading. Tuck the warp ends in and hem. The fringe is double, looped, with a neat reversible hem on both sides.

Sewn-on Fringed Edge

An easy way to make a different fringe effect is to alternate light and dark colors and two different spins in a fringe woven in a long strip (figure 4-25). The fringe, woven as a separate band, can be sewn on with a decorative stitch. Two wefts alternate—a darker, overspun yarn that curls up to a shorter length than a more loosely spun one, which casually twists on itself—to form a self-levelling fringe.

Fabricated and Applied Fringe

If you are not comfortable wearing a "fringey" fringe, this discreet edge might appeal to you and give you an idea (figure 4-26). It is also a good one to trim a nonwoven fabric that cannot be fringed. For a machine-knit jacket, Rilla Warner devised this fringe, made from woven cloth and stitched on with zigzag machine stitch. Wefts in a strip of woven linen were unwoven. Figure 4-27 shows how a double layer can be made by unweaving a length of cloth on each edge, leaving a few rows in the center for a heading. The cloth is folded over and zigzag-stitched to the edge (when folding, make one layer shorter than the other). For less bulk, the jacket is edged with a single layer of the linen fringe. Your choice of double or single layer will depend upon how full you want the fringe. When sewn with an embroidery stitch, the folded edge might be best. On a heavy handwoven textile, perhaps the single layer would be a better way, with a close zigzag or covering hand-stitch.

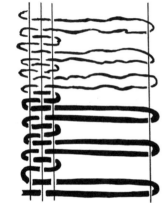

A

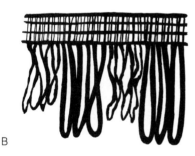

B

4-25. A two-level fringe. The yarns of different spins find their own level, with one curling up and the other gently twisting. (A) shows how to weave fringe over a skeleton or gauge warp, confining the selvedge every other row; and (B) illustrates alternating colors and spins.

4-26. A jacket with linen strip fringe all around. Notice how easily it follows the curves at the neckline and on the pockets. (By Rilla Warner, Tacoma, Washington; photograph by Beverly Rush)

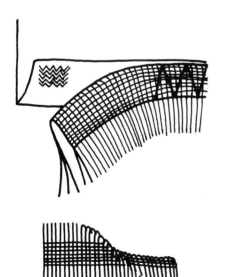

4-27. How a strip fringe of linen cloth is applied to a commercially knitted fabric.

TASSELS

Tassels are used for decoration . . . for fun . . . for elegance . . . for finishing . . . for pomp . . . for show of rank and power . . . for significance . . . because yarn ends are there!

Tassels are used worldwide and are centuries old. Historically, tassels have fulfilled a need for embellishment and symbolism. Designing and fabricating tassels is fun. They are fun to see— bouncy or dignified. A tassel can provide the exact punctuation mark at the tip of a hood, the end of a sash, the corners of a pillow, or the end of a bellpull; it can be used to decorate a bridle, accent the edge of a wall piece or a banner, or it can stand on its own (figure 4-28).

Tassels appear everywhere and there are as many ways to fashion them as there are places

4-28. An intricate, fascinating tassel from old China. Embroidery (Chinese knot stitch) is worked on the colorful butterfly shape; the tassel has wrapping, fanciful knots, and long silk strands. (From the collection of Beverly Rush; photograph by Beverly Rush)

4-29. We hung a tassel display on a fir tree in our yard to photograph a lot of them for you to see. Because I was tassel-minded, our next Christmas tree trim was all little tassels made from ready-cut yarn for knotted rugs on canvas. All colors were used.

to put them. They are so fascinating and endless in scope of method and use that I had to sternly call a halt and continue with my other chapters and embellishments. The methods and examples here are only a sampling of the possibilities. But the selections included here are representative of my own happy discoveries and experiments as well as of contributions from other cultures and other artisans.

Perhaps because the form of a tassel does resemble a person, the descriptive words used are usually head, neck, and skirt (sometimes, crown, collar, and body, or top, waistline, and skirt). The words I *usually* use are crown, collar (neck, when it is a long one!), and skirt. But whichever word is used, the meaning should be quite clear.

Weaving a Tassel

Two innovations in tassle-making evolved as I made dozens of them, using every method I could think of. Two schemes made the process easier, faster, less tedious, and added a broader range of design. The first was weaving a tassel. An intricately patterned collar is a bit tricky to do, so put warp on a loom for the skirt and crown, and weave the collar.

The collar of a tassel is a place for design and special ornamentation; and you don't have to use the traditional, predictable method of wrapping! It is difficult to weave a pattern around a hand-held bundle of yarn, so an easily controlled method of weaving the tassel is a logical step. Perhaps some of you have already found this out, but here is a way to do it (it led to some effects that were quite different for the crown and hangers).

All you need is a simple frame loom (figure 4-30). The frame should be long enough for the complete length of the tassel, including folded-in ends of the crown. Take the warps round and round the frame. This will give looped ends, if you wish, when you take the frame apart and slip the tassel off to cut. If cut ends are preferred at the top of the crown just cut the warp off from the loom. Wind on enough warps for the fullness desired. The width will depend on how luxuriously full your tassel is to be. If it is to be several inches wide, a solid tassel can be formed by rolling; if narrower, leave some longer weft ends in the weaving of the collar and then tie and sew them.

Weave back and forth across the approximate center of the warp for the collar. Make a band of any width, variety of yarns, colors, and weaving techniques. Greek or oriental soumak, basket weave, checkerboard (see tassels in C-2), stripes in either direction, and surface textures are just a few of the possibilities. Leave some weft ends for ties or for sewing the collar together.

There are many choices of what to do with the warps above the collar to make the crown of the tassel. In figure 4-30, groups of warp are being woven on the loom in plain weave in separate columns (the finished tassel to the left of the loom has warp groups woven in Greek soumak). Refer to the information on columns in chapter 2 for more ways to weave these crown warps, or leave them unwoven. This part becomes the crown of the tassel and can be finished off the loom in various ways. When weaving is finished, cut the tassel from the loom, or slip the frame out for loop ends, as suggested above.

Off the loom, the woven columns can be folded down with ends inside of the tassel crown. Roll

4-30. Weave a tassel on a frame loom: (right) groups of crown warps are being woven in plain-weave tabs; (left) a finished woven tassel with knotted warp crown tabs.

the collar section until the selvedges meet. Sew the seam or tie with weft ends. It may take a few tries to find just how much warp will make a full enough tassel; how wide to weave the band; and if it will just meet, need a center core, or be rolled so layers make a fatter tassel. A knotted or crocheted cord, or lengths of yarn, is run through the top loops of the crown. The hanger can be completed with a bow, bead, rings, self-loops, or whatever seems best.

Tassel Variations

My first woven tassel was too wide to make a full tassel when the selvedges were joined, so a tassel was put within a tassel. A small, plain-wrapped one of the same yarn as the woven tassel, with a yarn hanger tied on, was inserted in the center, with the top just above the turned-in warps. This made a chunky round, firm tassel. It is shown in the center, right, of figure 4-29.

My second innovative method of tassel-making is to use full skeins of yarn, as is—a real timesaver. They are already nicely coiled and ready for a collar, and they eliminate the tedium of winding off yarn and measuring (figure 4-31). Use small skeins of cotton embroidery floss and crewel wool, or the larger skeins of wool, approximately 40 yards.

Two more ideas will help in the process. First, wrap and knot the yarn of the collar in various ways so it is more stable and decorative than plain wrapping (figure 4-32). Second, look around for rings for slip-on ready-made collars. The collar on the large tassel in figure 4-31 is a ring woven of fine bamboo strips. Searching them out is an enjoyable pursuit. Look for scarf rings, small napkin rings, plain rings of jade, or curtain rings. Look in drapery hardware displays, in hardware stores, as well as in the other usual browsing places like antique shops, bead and findings stores, notion counters, and craft shops. Weave or braid narrow bands for collars. Discover and

4-31. Skein tassels—the quickest tassels in town! They are made from whole skeins of different yarns and sizes, ready measured and bunched. Beads, knots, and a bamboo ring are used as additions.

try! Be prepared to have tassels take over—the ideas and fabrication are habit-forming!

Tassels can also be made on a string-heddle jig. Braid or knot strands of yarn and form these into a loop with long ends (figure 4-32). Slip the ends through a large bead, knot a few times, then tie to the crown yarn on the peg. Wrap yarn round and round the pegs to the fullness wanted for the tassel. Wrap and tie the collar.

To form a tassel collar wrap-and-tie fashion, center a long wrapping length of yarn, bring ends up to the front, and tie a double knot, pulling the yarn in tightly. Next, wrap, tie, wrap, and tie until the collar is as wide as you need. The ends can be cut short after the final knots, or they can be darned in. This kind of collar will be firm and will stay in place. The line of knots adds an extra touch. Another version of the wrap-and-tie is to wrap short lengths, tied and with cut ends, one after the other for the width of the collar; this gives a fringed effect. Make many tassels at once by winding the skirt yarn over warping board pegs then cutting them apart.

For tiny tassels to make on your fingers, place a length of yarn for the hanging cord between your first two fingers (figure 4-33). Wrap the tassel yarn around your fingers until it is full enough. Tie the hanging cord in a double knot at the top loop. Remove from your fingers, flatten the coil of yarn down, and wrap and tie a cord around several times for a collar. These tassels could, of course, be embellished, but this very simple, basic result is appropriate when several of these small tassels are bundled up or are used to embellish larger tassels.

4-33. Three steps in making tiny tassels over your fingers—a fast, simple method when you need a lot of them.

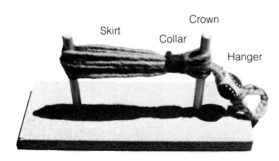

4-32. A tassel made over a jig for tying string heddles. It makes a nice-size tassel. The bead and hanging loop are knotted on first.

4-34. Tiny tassels bunched—Mexican style—at the back of a shaped belt. Two tassels are at each end of the narrowed tie in front.

4-35. Forms for tassel tops. A few hours spent browsing and pawing through boxes of wooden molds for tassel crowns at a tassel factory was a delight. They made tassels and buttons and cords for banners, uniforms, stage curtains, and what not. At the factory, they cover the forms smoothly with shiny fine threads. You could also stain or paint them.

4-37. An orange silk tassel, crowned with knotted netting, adorns a white porcelain bell from Japan. Note the simple loop attachment.

4-36. Chinese tassels. The tassels of very fine orange silk thread are formed over a cardboard cylinder. In the same method as for the edge on the Chinese purse in figure 2-25, the black thread is wound evenly around the cylinder, picking up the orange threads and weaving a pattern on the vertical (warp) threads of the tassel top. A simple twisted cord is the hanger. (From the collection of Beverly Rush)

More Tassel Ideas

Build tassels with combinations:

- Make round pom-poms to perch on top of a plain tassel.
- Thread yarns through beads for the crown or the collar.
- Start a tassel with a lark's-head hitch on a ring then add yarns.
- A small amount of yarn of a special spin or fiber will show off to good advantage in a tassel, and all of the beauty will be seen.
- Combine some of the dangles and pom-poms with straight yarns.
- Mask the crown with beads, embroidery stitches, or openwork knots.
- Knit a tube and slip it over the crown.
- While weaving a band, add little tassels along the edge. Prepare the small tassels as shown in figure 4-33, tying the hanger in then the collar. As you weave the band, weave in the hanger as the weft, first one strand then the other, so it will be fastened as part of the weaving in two rows. Space the tassels as you please—bunched or spread.
- A perky tassel is made by clustering small tassels into a crown. These flare out and are especially effective in a fine soft cotton, silk, or wool. It is much like the little silk "donkey" tassels from Italy often found at interior designers' studios.
- One more place to employ the knitted cord is for a tassel collar. Use one or two rows fastened on or a whole long neck of cords wrapped around for a ribbed effect. An unusual application might be to make a whole tassel skirt of knitted cords. Knit short cords (twice as long as the tassel would be), fold over, and wrap the collar around it.

Tibetan Ornament

The larger-than-life Tibetan ornament, shown in figures 4-38 and 4-39, qualifies as an embellishment, a tassel, a trim, or an accessory! It is of silk in deep rich colors—blues and reds—with the wrapped and woven ends held by a large round brass pin. This treasure, when found by Anita Mayer, was dull and soiled. After cleaning, it proved to be beautifully crafted and rich in color. She wears it with some of her handwoven robes of handspun and natural-dye yarns, a perfect foil for the elegant piece. The cord and

4-38. Detail of the Tibetan ornament in figure 4-1. The brass medallion that holds the tassels looks woven.

4-39. The woven Turk's-head rings are like the ones on the Chinese tassel in figure 4-28.

fringe at the bottom are black. The Turk's-head rings on the strands are just like the ones on the ancient Chinese tassel in figure 4-28.

Comparisons are inevitable in studying ornaments from different cultures. The four different treatments of the separate strands are similar to some of the large ornamental woven and fringed pieces found in Peru. The encirclement of the groups just below the four wrapped sections appears to be much like some of the pom-poms and dangles found on Bolivian coca bags. This effect can be achieved by stacking up rings (figure 4-42). The tight wrapping on the loose strands at the bottom is much like tassels from various Asian countries.

Pom-Poms

Pom-poms are fun, soft, colorful, and appealing. We see them on baby and ski caps, fancy packages, key rings, clown suits, and crowning tassels. Cluster them on corners, edges, and ends. I equate them with Acacia blossoms, dandelion puffs, exotic seed pods, and milkweed pods.

4-40. Sewing-thread-size cotton warps in black and light brown are caught and wrapped into full tassels below a knotted fringe. Smoothly clipped pom-poms are suspended through the centers. (Photograph by Kent Kammerer)

4-41. A white wool tie from Mexico with pom-pom tassels and a cluster of brightly colored wrapped discs. (Courtesy, Anita Mayer)

Borrow the colors and textures from natural things and from other cultures. The Mexican and Guatemalan craftsmen have a way with warp ends, tassels, and pom-poms that is distinctive and handsome. The extremely fine stranded cotton floss they use provides full warp ends for elaborate knotted fringe patterns and tassels—with round pom-poms added. In figure 4-40, a rebozo-like knotted fringe on warps of very fine black and light brown cotton ends in warp groups is gathered into full tassels. A smooth, round pom-pom is fastened up through the middle of the tassel. On the white Mexican tie shown in figure 4-41, twisted and tasseled ends are the reverse of those in figure 4-40, with the pom-poms as the crown. Combine the round clipped balls with simple tassels in different ways.

Wheeled Edges

Ethnic costumes and textiles are such fun to study when you note all of the many special touches of embroidery and construction. Part of a Laotian costume (C-4), a long wide sash of black cotton, has a colorful section at each end. So much is going on here, all in a space about 24" wide and up from each end about 18". The following detailed description will help you become aware of all the different design factors.

The whole long piece is hand-hemmed with a narrow rolled hem. At the corners, a folded red cotton binding is sewn with a row of minute chain stitch and tiny close overcast stitches on the outer edge. At each corner, the binding is decoratively knotted before continuing up the edge. Where the binding ends, four small embroidered wheels are fastened. Three have

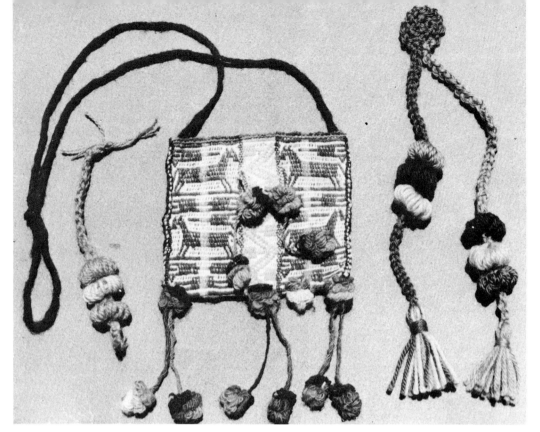

4-42. Coca bag (chuspa) with pom-poms in layers of loosely wrapped cords. The little secret pocket in the woven detached section is in the center with two clusters. On either side are my versions of the pom-pom, attached to crocheted cords.

"necks" and the fourth one is sewn onto the end of the binding. Next come a few inches of triangular stitches; at first glance, they all look like a pointed blanket stitch—some of them are— but a closer look shows that some are worked with a long and short stitch, caught into the stitches at the edge. All of the stitches are in cotton or silk sewing-thread size in several colors. The slim rows of chain stitch, placed so they cross at the corners, are spaced in an interesting way. The final, subtle touch is that some rows are chained on one side, others on the reverse, so that on each face, some rows look like tiny running stitches and others are the fine chain. Now *that* is designing with a simple stitch!

The wheels are intriguing. A form is covered with red cloth, then triangles are embroidered through to the other side so they are identical. The thread is taken through the cloth at the edge (leaving a rim of cloth) and through the center (making an eyelet). The cloth smoothly covers the edge, with no obvious seam or wrinkle—a small mystery. The whole piece is completely reversible and neatly finished on both sides. It was purchased at the Textile Museum Shop, Washington, D.C., and the only information on it said it was made by a Black Tai woman from Laos. This lengthy description is shared with you because of my delight in finding so many different techniques and how they were used on this fairly simple piece, and also to encourage you to really study textiles thoroughly for rewarding finds.

Wrapped Pom-Pom and Wrapped Edge

My all-time favorite—and of those who have learned it—is the wrapped ball and edge. The core could be a round bead with a large hole, a styrofoam ball, a wooden form, or a small cork float bobber, but I much prefer a yarn ball—it takes little time, the material is at hand (use unwanted, ugly yarns!), and it has good traction to hold the wrapping.

4-43. How to wrap the warps wound around the yarn ball core. This is similar to the wrapped edge in figures 2-29 and 2-30.

4-44. Several appropriate techniques were employed in this large tote-bag (C-10), including the wrapped pom-pom idea from a small coca bag (C-9). Along the top edge, the warp ends are brought over to the top side and wrapped and twisted. Wrapped pom-poms dangle all around the bottom edge. A long, narrow tapestry-weave band, like the Mexican hair ties, is sewn up the side seam, the long length continuing for a shoulder strap, then sewn down the other side. The construction is especially suitable for a heavy wool bag. The firm cotton cloth lining is the bag, with sewn bottom. This method keeps the outer layer from being distorted by pulling in if it was closed along the bottom. (Designer/weaver, Polly Matsumoto, Sanibel Island, Florida)

Study figure 4-43 to see how the final turns around the yarn core are wound so you have warps from top to bottom, which are wrapped. Leave a small space between these "warps" for the wrapping yarn. With a long tapestry needle, start each wrapping yarn by running through the ball from bottom to top. Leave ends out for hangers at the top and bottom, for tie-ons, or for further embellishments; or, as in the wrapped balls in figure 2-29, just take a stitch or two to secure the end and run it inside, with no extra ends showing. Keep the wrapping even and smooth, but not taut. Each wrap should just touch the previous one. Use a different color for each segment, or have them match. A smooth spin gives a more defined look to the sections, but almost any yarn is suitable. Very fine yarns tend to result in less smooth wrapping; medium weights wools, like crewel or knitting worsted, are very satisfactory. Finishing of the top and bottom is your choice; use braids, knots, several strands separated and wrapped, ring loops, or whatever strikes your fancy.

EMBELLISHMENT

An embellishment is an ornament or trim, or a trim, plus. It includes tassels on tassels, beads, buttons, and bows on trimming bands. Embroidery stitches can encrust a surface, every part with special touches. Some pieces have so many different techniques, colors, weaves, and finishes that I have placed them under the heading of embellishment. Figure 4-45 shows woven overshots with needlework added.

To an almost unimaginable degree, richness was an integral part of royal burials in cultures where treasures were provided for an afterlife.

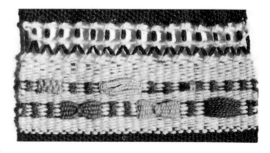

4-45. Embellishments in the form of woven overshots. These long wefts become warps that are woven or knotted for surface texture.

A Chinese dowager empress was wrapped nine times around with a single strand of matched pearls; her robe and coverlet, heavy with jewels, were just a part of the opulence. Mummies of Egyptian Pharoahs were incredibly embellished with gold and jewels. Coronation and royal robes through the centuries are fascinating examples of adornment. Japanese obis are exquisitely embroidered (C-6). Today, a heavily embroidered bodice or border seems modest in comparison, but the desire to add some richness and handwork is strong. It certainly has deep authentic roots in history. One dictionary defines "embroider" as "anything pleasant but unimportant." I hope this refers only to exaggerated verbal or written details—not to adornment by needlework!

A variety of embroidery uses and stitches follow. These examples are meant to give you ideas and ways to make use of stitches. Refer to the many stitches detailed in chapter 3. Most of those are surface stitches, adapted as joins, but you can also use them for enrichment. The vast number of books on embroidery will be helpful, too.

Shisha Embroidery

Shisha embroidery (figures 4-47 and C-1) is composed of shiny discs held in place by various embroidery stitches, buttonhole stitches, and other familiar stitches. Scattered, open designs or stitches worked around the circles to completely cover the surface, all in glowing colors, are used on saris, clothing, hats, and household textiles.

Shawl from India

Multiple methods are combined in a brightly colored shawl from India (figures 4-47 and C-1). The basic textile is handwoven white wool that has been tie-dyed red-purple, with tiny dots of the original white remaining. It is lined with a printed silk, which is brought over the edge around the neck—a thoughtful idea to protect the skin from scratchy wool. A wide band of embroidery stitches, including shisha embroidery, all in a flowery pattern, is next. Then, along the edge, techniques that relate to weaving are worked: rows of oriental soumak, if woven, or outline stitches, if embroidered; a narrow row of

4-46. Small embroidered silk purse from old China. Details of the unusual border techniques and the exquisite embroidery are shown in figure 2-25. (From the collection of Beverly Rush)

4-47. Detail of a shawl from Gujerat, India. Also see C-1. (Courtesy, Leslie Grace, Folk Art Gallery, La Tienda, Seattle, Washington)

openwork with warps wrapped; and more rows of the soumak/outline stitch. The wefts in each row of the stitches are extended beyond the selvedge, braided, and tasseled. The final grand touch along the bottom edge is a row of miniature tassels, tightly packed and all hitched together. The shawl is an intriguing study of the use of color, textures, and techniques.

Algerian Eye Stitch

The Algerian eye stitch is composed of straight stitches (figure 4-50), each one radiating out from the center. Properly done, there should be eight stitches worked in a square. Since each stitch is slightly pulled as it goes out from the center, a hole or eye is formed. In our informal use of this stitch on a shawl, some were worked in squares to echo the small square of the weave, and some were worked into circles.

4-48. Mary Ann Spawn's richly embellished handbags are becoming collector's items. They are of the finest velvets and silks and are beautifully embroidered and designed. The velvet and embroidery on this one is further adorned with silk tassels. (Artist, Mary Ann Spawn, Tacoma, Washington; photograph by Beverly Rush)

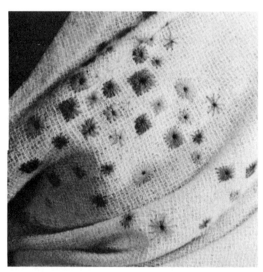

4-49. More embellishment by embroidery. On a white wool tabard, a rounded meandering pattern of embroidery and silver circles blends with the shapes in the edge stitch of handspun wool (Eskimo lacing stitch, see figures 2-27 and 2-28). Small silver circles are part of the side closures.

4-50. Embroidery on a shawl. The triangular shawl, cut from handloomed fine white wool, is embellished with embroidered squares and circles at random. Just one stitch is used—the Algerian eye stitch—in very fine light-colored wool yarns. It is a subtle way to fill a surface with stitches varying in size and color. The hem is shaped and sewn with closed herringbone stitch (figure 2-67). The other two edges are unadorned, with a few wefts pulled to make a short, straight fringe. A crepelike spin of two fine wools used in the weaving keeps the weft from raveling out. But, if it should ravel, a narrow hem, herringboned, can be put in.

Woven-in Embellishment

Woven patterns might be called an embellishment. A border, a woven-on band, an elaborate edge as part of the weaving, or figures or accents of another technique all qualify as embellishment, especially if they are further ornamented and augmented by stitches. You can find examples of this throughout the book. The Guatemalan weaving in figure 4-52 is also included to show one way of disposing of pattern weft ends in a most natural, honest way. Simply weave the beginning and ending weft ends out from the figures. It is tidier than tucking in on a fine cotton weave, and the effect becomes a natural part of a weaving style—a distinctive part of the weaving. These ends even have a name: "streamers." This example substantiates my credo: if you can't gracefully dispose of awkward ending lengths of weft, design them in! Let them remain on the surface or at the selvedge, or weave them in as Guatemalan streamers.

The next chapter adds practical and imaginative ways with buttons and ties.

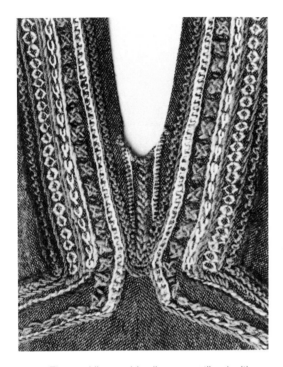

4-51. The neckline and bodice are outlined with rows and rows of stitches on a vintage (made in 1950!) handwoven brown and gray wool dress. The stitches are in natural handspun wool (grays and white) and crewel wool (soft gray blue). The lines emphasize the cut of the bodice. Stitches are familiar ones: outline, buttonhole, Y, raised chain band, and cross stitch flowers in handspun wools. At the V of the neckline, a reinforcement of buttonhole stitch is on the edge. (Photograph by Beverly Rush)

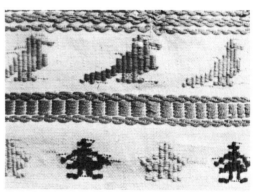

4-52. Guatemalan weaving embellished with birds and figures. The beginning and ending of laid-in wefts are frankly woven in as "streamers," a characteristic part of their design.

5. Closures

Closures are usually needed for wearing apparel. Household weavings need closures, too—pillow covers, for example. The suggestions and methods that follow can be used for both.

Fastening a garment at front, neck, or sleeve is often necessary, but the method and material can be an interesting challenge, especially for a handweaver. Complete some during the weaving; begin others to be completed later. To compose a whole design, you must consider the substance and type of closure needed, but it must work efficiently, too. Prime considerations are ease of use and durability. One of the most suitable and practical closures is woven wefts extended at the selvedge as ties (figure 5-5), another is woven slits for lacing or buttonholes. Any integral closure—such as woven-in loops, slits, ties, or buttons—will withstand the constant moving and tugging much better than something sewn on. When designing, keep this in mind.

Examples of these methods give you only a brief look at the possible solutions. Each project and yarn will suggest a preferred or logical method. Found objects can become a feature, with sea shells (figure 5-3), bone, horn, driftwood, and other gleanings from Mother Nature adapted to useful purposes. Look, scrounge, discover, try out; study costumes from other cultures, other

ages. The necessity of closing and opening a garment has been met in elaborate or simple ways. Tying and lacing are direct and logical.

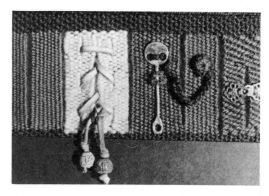

5-1. From unit 9 on the scroll, preparations for closures. From left to right are: firm, straight selvedges for closure examples; woven slits for lacing with a leather thong; two horizontal loops woven in to hold the brass pick; a knotted cord fastened to the pick; a loop at the end of the cord slips over the crocheted button to make an easily fastened closure; and a small pewter clasp from Norway, an appropriate closure, with one half sewn on each side of the opening.

5-2. An eclectic assortment of buttons and other pieces for closures or embellishment. Most of these are hand-fashioned from clay, metal, or wood.

Buttons and snaps and hooks are secure and satisfactory. The fun comes in exercising your own ingenuity to provide an appropriate closure where required.

ASSEMBLED CLOSURES

Figure 5-2 shows an assemblage of materials that can be used for closures: handmade buttons, of wood or clay; pewter clasps and buttons; sea urchin spines; horse hardware from a tack shop; tapestry bobbins; and an ancient Japanese ivory mask button. The advent of macramé as a popular craft was followed by a deluge of large clay and wood beads suitable for fasteners, tassel tops, and cord finales on handwovens. Other findings that can be used in many ways are tiny brass bells; wooden or metal rings; extra-large hooks and eyes; thread-covered hooks-and-eyes used on furs; and toggle fastenings of leather and wood. I have a lovely bent, rusted, squared nail, either from our old dock or from a plank that drifted in. So far, it has not seemed just right for part of a closure, but it might appear on a rough homespun jacket!

Shells with natural holes from which the host was plucked by a marauder are naturals for dangles on ties and lacings; or holes can be carefully drilled in. The slide fastening on the sash of a batik dress shown in figure 5-3 is a section of a shell from Hawaii. Buttons sliced from deer horns are nature's gift to handweavers and knitters. Nutshells cut in two for buttons are three-dimensional sculptures (figure 5-4).

Several forms and colors of dried Eucalyptus pods are right with natural wools. Some look like polished wood, others are textured cone shapes of gray green. Nature is a supermarket for fiber workers—from inspiration for textures and color

5-3. Sash from a batik dress fashioned in Hawaii is appropriately fastened by a section of a Hawaiian shell. The two ends of cloth slip through the large hole.

5-4. Sliced nutshell buttons are successful on a woolen handwoven coat. (By Jean Sullivan, Seattle, Washington)

to objects to use. Searching is more than half the fun. You may find—or be—a craftsman who can design and make just-right final finishes for your handwovens.

Designing for Simplicity

Sometimes no closure at all is the best solution for a garment. When a vest or coat fits well and hangs nicely in place, buttons or ties may be redundant. The linen vest shown in figure 2-66 was to have two silver circles and a knotted cord tie. The rows and rows of embroidery made it seem like an unnecessary detail, so nothing interrupts the lines of stitches.

Household and Decorative Weavings

This chapter deals mostly with closures for clothing, but some of the ideas are adaptable to household or decorative weavings.

Button a pillow cover on for easy removal for cleaning. The detachable sleeve idea works well on a pillow cover (figure 5-7). Weave the loops in along one edge, sew buttons onto the other, then wrap the cover around the pillow form and button up! Or weave slits, then lace or button the edges together (figure 5-1). Tying weft or warp ends together is discussed in chapter 3, with joinings. When the weft ends are tied and the ends left on the surface, a row of instant fringe trim is made along one edge. If the weft ends are tucked back inside as they are tied, a decorative row of knots is the trim. A tied join is quite easily untied, then tied together again, making it a practical closure. Any of the above will serve as a trimming feature, and will complete a handcrafted product.

A knitted, crocheted, or knotted cord and a large button arrangement will hold pulled-back drapery. Or weave bands with loops or slits at each end to slip over a hook. Lengthen a curtain (or garment) by buttoning on a deep hem. Slits or loops are woven for the attachment. Lace with thongs or cords instead of buttoning.

LOOPS AND BUTTONS

Buttoning on, weaving loops, and variations on these themes are ideas that bloom and grow. Preparation for buttons and buttonholes, no matter how they will be used or placed, is basically the same. Don't forget that careful measuring and allowance for weaving take-up and shrinkage is necessary when the fastening must come at the right place.

Weave rows of weft that extend into loops. The number of woven rows between the extended wefts is determined by the size loop needed. Loops can lie close to the selvedge, move out and back at the same spot, or loop out and back in a large arc to fit a large button. The loops should be buttonhole-stitched or chained for strength and wear. The loop weft doesn't have to be the full width of your cloth; it can start a few inches from the edge (figure 5-5). Use matching yarn if a stripe is not part of the design.

Weave slits along the selvedge. Make them several warps in so the buttons or laces won't pull and distort them. In figure 5-1 the slits were made three warp ends in. If slits are to be embroidered as an accent, as in figure 5-11, do this on the loom, as the weaving progresses. Off the loom, crochet edges with loops; sew on a band that has been woven with slits; or chain stitch loops.

Figure 5-5 shows four different sizes of loops and woven-in ties. In A the weft is chained over the warp from left to right, continued out beyond the selvedge, and chained "in the air." The weft is then returned and chained over the warp from right to left. The loop is round because the rows are directly above each other. In B, the loop is long and close to the selvedge, with the chained rows separated by fifteen rows of plain weave. At the selvedge, a small loop, C, is made by weaving in the loop weft, extending it out beyond the selvedge, and dropping it while seven rows of the main weft are woven. The loop weft is then returned and woven in, leaving a small loop. This loop is then covered with buttonhole stitch. Take care to begin and end the stitches with several overcast stitches around the selvedge. The long, slim loop, D, is sewn to the selvedge with several overcast stitches. Loop the yarn out, and work buttonhole stitches over it. This method is not quite as secure as the woven-in versions. The woven-in ties are three lengths of tie weft that is woven in an inch or more in the same shed as the main weft. If a stripe is not desirable, use matching yarn. The long ends are knotted three times, snugging them close to the selvedge, then braided. A tie woven in on the opposite edge makes a tied join at the front of a garment, or ties for an underarm join.

Raspberry Buttons

Buttons may be sewn on or, better yet, woven in, as shown in figure 5-6; or needle the ends through the cloth and tie them on. Weft rows of chaining over the warps continue out in a chain (use a crochet hook) and return to make button loops. These "raspberry" buttons are crocheted (see below); leave two long ends to be knotted with two overhand knots for a short shank. The two ends are woven in, over and under four warps, with the button right at the edge. To make this closure a little different, the loops and buttons alternate on each edge. When all are unbuttoned, an interesting edge trim shows. This requires some measuring to ensure that both sides align evenly. The whole process is finished on the loom. If two sections of a garment are being woven at one time (with two shuttles, and on a wide loom), it is easy to get the spacing even. In the example shown here, there are ten rows of plain weave between the woven chain rows. Seven "in the air" chain stitches form the loops. Alternate buttons and loops as shown

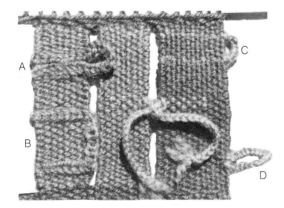

5-5. Detail of scroll, unit 6, showing four different sizes of loops and woven-in ties.

here, or put buttons on one edge and loops on the other. A suggestion hesitantly offered to a weaver: the pom-pom-and-loop braid sold for café and shower curtains provides a fast way to acquire a button and loop fastening. Sew a strip along each edge, then button across.

There are several ways to crochet raspberry buttons. These are fairly soft buttons, but can be made more firm by inserting a small round button or a wad of yarn before drawing up and knotting the ends. Note: choose or make the buttons before making the loops, so they will fit. Make a knot with a small loop, leaving a few inches of yarn for sewing on, tying on, or weaving in. Crochet three chain stitches, go back into chain two, and single crochet around and around into each chain until the button is the size required. Keep the knot and end in the center so it will be in place to tie with the last end for the shank—coming out of the bottom of the ball. The rows will cup. Lock the last stitch by pulling the end through the loop and cut, leaving a length for attaching. Tie the beginning and finishing ends together in several overhand knots to make a shank. Pull the knots very tightly; this

5-6. Woven weft chain continues into crocheted chain loops. Crochet buttons are woven in for security. Buttons and loops alternate from side to side.

forms the round ball. Just before knotting the ends together, insert a form or some yarn ends to firm the button up, if necessary. Twenty-four inches of tapestry wool makes a button about one-half inch across and high when you use a size H or 6 crochet hook.

Detachable Sleeves

Delving into costume design, studying ancient portraits of the gentry, and examining medieval tapestries is always rewarding, especially when a new use for a textile or stitch is found. The ancients apparently respected the value of talent and effort and used parts of beautifully worked costumes again and again. Ornately embroidered, quilted, beaded, or ruffled sleeves were fashioned and put into other garments, saved and treasured, and then used again. An earlier and different practice was saving and reapplying the fine tapestry bands and roundels of the Coptic weavers, cut from the original tunic when it became worn.

In this day of moving swiftly from climate to climate, it is helpful to add or subtract from one garment. Of course the obvious way is to dress in layers—sleeveless garments with the addition of a blouse, sweater, or jacket—but it is fun to design and put together an innovative solution.

A number of years ago, before our present-day practice of wearing anything anywhere, a fashion period decreed short skirts or long skirts for specific occasions. At that time, I devised some ways of adding or subtracting a deep hem to lengthen or shorten a skirt instantly. It still seems a good idea to give multipurpose wear. The need for adaptable handwoven clothing led to the in-and-out sleeve idea.

A handwoven cotton dress in a medium color range, with detachable sleeves, can go from a cool fall or winter to warm tropics, looking and feeling right in either place (from Seattle to Hawaii, for example). We asked around for completed examples, and have one very good one to illustrate.

Judy Thomas worked out a handsome and practical solution (figure 5-7). Hers was a very heavy handspun wool, but the basic plan can apply to a lighter weight, with smaller loops and buttons, a narrower, smaller sleeve, capelike or slim. Soft crocheted or flat buttons in a matching color would be a subtle trim. Bold and flashy buttons and embroidered or woven patterns would put emphasis on the sleeve and shoulder. The illustration shows the sleeveless tunic with button trim—without the cape sleeve and with it buttoned on. The squared neckline and armhole are shaped on the loom. Button loops are a continuation of the weft stripe beyond the selvedge, making the loop, and back to the selvedge about an inch above, with darker plain weave in between. The ends of the handspun wool make small bumps along the opposite selvedge. The tunic is woven sideways, so the selvedge at the bottom is the finish—no hem is needed.

The same result can be achieved with a crochet hook, either off the loom on the cloth, or on the loom as weaving progresses (figure 5-6). Crocheted loops can also be added to the edges of a vest for a knitted cord lacing. In figure 5-8, the loops and cord are fashioned from the same

5-8. Loops crocheted on the edges of a vest. A knitted cord of the same llama wool is used for a lacing and small Mexican spindle whorls are on the ends.

5-7. Deep capelike sleeves button on to a sleeveless tunic. (Designer/weaver Judy Thomas, Woodinville, Washington)

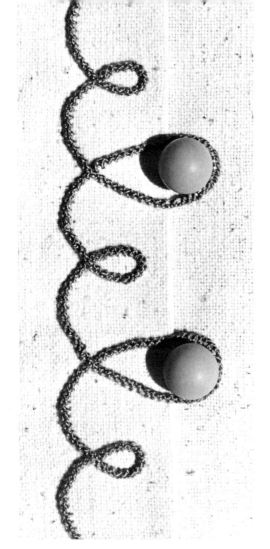

5-9. Palestrina knot stitch is couched over a cord on the cloth. The buttonhole loops are a continuation of the stitch over the cord only. (By Sue Roach; photograph by Beverly Rush)

llama yarn, and ancient drop-spindle whorls embellish the cord ends. In figure 5-9, an airy line of Palestrina knot stitches, worked over a cord, spirals on the cloth and moves out into a button loop. The rows of chain stitch or other stitches don't always *have* to be straight! Palestrina knot stitch is shown in Figure 3-47.

Slit-weave Buttonholes

Knowing how to weave a proper slit is a must if you plan to have woven buttonholes. A woven slit is a space between warps, with selvedge on each edge. It is the slit weave that is part of the plain-weave tapestry and Kelim techniques. Practice weaving slits on a reference/sampler (figure 5-10). It takes some experience to weave a slit with straight and even tension. A useful slit should have straight, firm selvedges. It can be slightly widened into an oval by a gradual tightening of the weft, or both edges can just touch.

To weave, use two bobbins, one for each side. When the slit is the size you need, close the top by continuing with the full-width weft and one shuttle. Set the slits a few warps in from the selvedge (figure 5-1). The strain of lacing or buttoning will pull the slits out of shape if they are too close to the edge (figure 5-11). A tailor's guide for placement of a buttonhole is a button-width from the edge. Accurate measurement is required, especially when there are several slits for garment closures.

Tabs woven with slits in them can be woven beyond the selvedge, or woven separately and sewn on. The weft tabs in figure 2-2 could be woven long enough for a side closure, with a buttonhole slit to fasten a button on the opposite edge.

A small embroidered patch with a buttonhole worked in can be put on top of a woven buttonhole slit and be held in place with the button that goes through both. These have been seen on jackets from Guatemala, and are a way of changing an embellishment or removing it, as desired. A felt or leather patch around a buttonhole and/or under a button, sewn with embroidery stitches, reinforces as well as decorates.

Make a feature of the slit for a closure by including a spot of woven pattern or embroidery around it. Judy Wick closed the sides of a fine wool tabard (figure 5-11) by drawing slender leather thongs through between warps and tying them in a bow. The slits were surrounded by a pattern that echoed the woven overshot design at the neckline. The slits should have been placed a few warps in from the edge; so close, they tend to pull while worn.

For centuries, camel saddlebags (C-2) have been closed with a tight and quite easily manipulated closure—a cord chained through slits. The system works equally well on handbags or garments. Along the edge of one side, buttonhole slits are woven or worked. On the opposite side, a sturdy cord is sewn with spaced loops (figure 5-12). The loops are sized to reach to and through

5-10. Slits—all sizes and placements, from the reference/sampler scroll, unit 7. Bars and vertical loops can be used for belts or scarves.

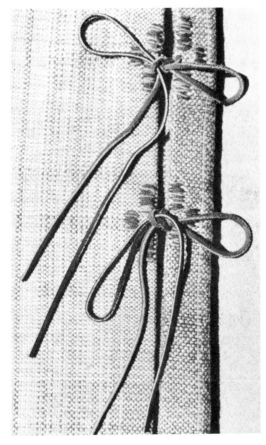

5-11. An effective and simple closure on the sides of a tabard. Slim leather thongs are slipped through between warps surrounded by a bit of pattern like the overshot pattern woven at the neckline. (Weaver, Judy Wick, Portland, Oregon)

5-12. Pakistani saddle blanket closure on a wool and leather cape. Slits are woven in one edge, the crochet cord is sewn to the other edge. To close, the cord is chained through the slits. (Designer/weaver, Luanna Sever, Tacoma, Washington; photograph by Beverly Rush)

5-13. Ring and cord closure for the front of a jacket of the handwoven cotton in the background. It is made from the same pearl cotton in the weaving.

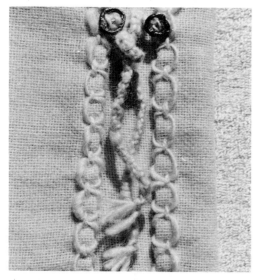

5-14. Silver circles hold the knotted cords at the sides of a white wool tabard. See figure 4-49 for embellishment at the neckline. (Silver circles by Kit Gifford, Queen Charlotte Islands)

5-15. Beads as lacing loops. Beads are strung on the outside row of Palestrina knot stitch. (By Sue Roach; photograph by Beverly Rush)

the next loop easily, without puckering. To close, bringing the two sides together; each loop in turn is drawn through each slit, and the loops are then chained together. A button, preferably a firm crocheted one, is sewn at the end for the last loop to lock the chain. A closing that withstands the sands and winds of the desert in a camel train should be secure enough for almost any use!

Cords Plus

Cords can be braided, knotted, crocheted, or twisted. As closures, they are used with rings, loops, slits, or buttons, or they can be flat buttons with long ends (figure 5-16).

A jacket closure is shown on the textile in figure 5-13. The cords and rings are in the same yellow, beige, and orange pearl cotton used in the weaving. The plastic rings are covered with the tailor's buttonhole stitch (figure 3-22), which has an extra ridged edge. Unit 9 on the scroll (figure 1-3) has two covered rings for a tied closure. For the cord, doubled strands are hitched over the rings, then braided and wrapped; they are then divided into two ends with tassels, which is typical of finishes on tasseled camel trappings and some Mexican hair ties and belts.

In figure 5-14, small silver rings sewn to the side edge of a tabard hold the tie cords. The over-the-edge stitch is Eskimo lacing (figures 2-27 and 2-28). The ties are double strands of the same handspun wool used for the edge stitch, knotted with overhand knots, alternating direction (also see figure 4-49).

Figure 5-15 shows a clever use of beads as lacing loops. Two rows of Palestrina knot stitch (figure 3-47) are worked at the edge of the neck opening. Beads are strung on at intervals in the second row of stitches and a twisted cord is laced through.

On a long rectangular tunic (figure 5-16), just one point of closure is made. Coiled buttons are formed of twisted cord, which continues into long ends. The buttons are sewn at the edge, front and back, to come just under the arm; the armholes are created when the long cords are knotted and hang free on the open sides. The cords are made from the same colorful silk woven in the pattern.

5-16. Tied cords close the sides of a long tunic, high up, just under the arm. (Weaver, Joan Walker)

Vertical Loop

Horizontal and vertical loops or bars, added as you weave or put in with needle and yarn later, are shown in figures 5-1 and 5-10. If just one warp is sufficient for a vertical loop, lift it up and buttonhole stitch for the length needed, drop it back, and continue weaving. An easy way to do this is to weave across the whole warp skipping the loop warp (two at the most) for the length you want. Then buttonhole stitch along the raised warp. If you require a loop that is more than two warps wide, extra warps are added, as seen at the center of figure 5-10 (if you pick up too many warps from the weaving itself, it will make a thin spot). Add the extra warp ends from the back, carry them up over the weaving to the length needed, then down through and fasten at the back. Be very careful to secure all of the ends by needling in, as these loops may have much wear. Weave back and forth on these extra warps.

Horizontal Bars

If horizontal bars are required, as in the closure in figure 5-1, these can be added while weaving or afterward with a needle and yarn. One or more strands of yarn are fastened across for the width needed, then they are buttonhole stitched. If just a few of these closures are used, they are more easily placed after the garment is put together.

Cords and Picks

The flexible knitted cord, which can be made on as few as three stitches in fine yarn, is appropriate for the cord-and-pick closures such as those in figures 5-1 and 5-18. Instructions for knitting the cords are in chapter 4, page 103. When one or two horizontal bars are woven or stitched on both sides of a coat front, the whole assembly of two picks and the cord can be lifted out when the garment is worn with no closures. The small bars in matching yarn are not too noticeable. The picks can be of any suitable material or shape. In the assemblage of closures, figure 5-2, are several ideas. I like to use tapestry bobbins; horseshoe nails also work well and are a conversation piece!

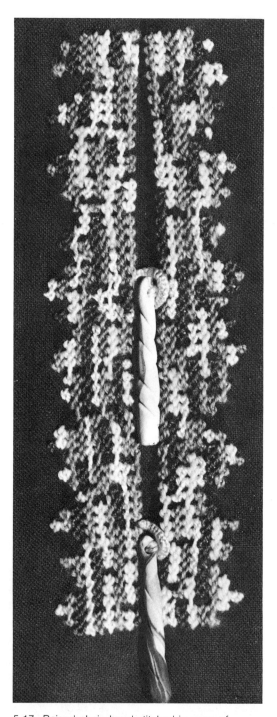

5-17. Raised chain band stitched in rows, of several colors. The closure is buttonholed rings with twisted clay forms slipped through. See the sea urchin spines in figure 5-2; these can have a hole bored through for the same purpose. (By Sue Roach)

Closures to Find or Make

A plastron of raised chain band stitches (figure 5-17), buttonholed loops, and long twists of clay can be combined for an unusual and very decorative neckline fastening. Also see the sea urchin spines at the end of the second band from the left in figure 5-2; they have holes bored through the top to make fanciful ends on lacing cords or sashes.

If you are a weaver, use wooden weaving tools for closures. Slender, graceful tapestry bobbins are ideal for picks in loop-and-pick closures. A jacket idea is shown in figure 5-18. Several strands of wool are sewn in one huge Sorbello stitch on one side (figure 3-35). The ends are left several inches long and are knotted. On the opposite side, a few strands are sewn into a horizontal bar. The tapestry bobbin is slipped through, and the ends from the opposite side are wound around for a closing simple to operate. The bobbin could have been tied to the ends and then dropped through the bar; this is how the brass pick was fastened in figure 1-3. Two tapestry bobbin shapes are shown in the collection in figure 5-2. One bobbin is sewn to the cloth and the ends wrapped around a large wooden button on the opposite side. One or a pair of the lovely little carved and beaded lace-maker bobbins would be a jewellike closure or trim.

5-18. Closure for a weaver. A tapestry bobbin, strands of wool yarn, and one queen-size Sorbello stitch.

5-19. Narrow folded cloth tie in the style of ties on Japanese Hippari jackets. Open cretan stitch is on both sides.

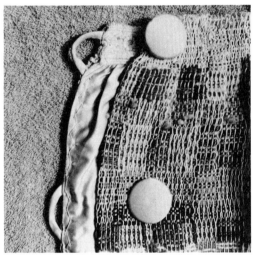

5-20. Covered buttons, loops, and lining are all of the same light blue satin, a foil for the textured weave in light colors. Note the wide brocade ribbon inside the drawn-up weft waistband, and the herringbone stitch on the lining. (Weaver, Joan Walker, Redmond, Washington)

Folded lengths of cloth can be sewn into narrow, flat ties or cording. In figure 5-19, the tie is sewn with cretan stitch (figure 3-28) in the style of a Japanese Hippari jacket. The stitch is on both sides of the tie so it looks finished however tied. The textile is a very fine cotton, loomed in Japan.

There are some very nice finishing details in the multicolored cotton wrap skirt shown in figure 5-20. The waistband is formed by drawing up rows of weft. This is a good treatment to remember when just a little bit of gathering is suitable. The band is firm, and the sewn-on band

5-21. An assortment of buttons made on bone rings in crochet and buttonhole stitch variations. Each one has a tail of thread for sewing on. (By Mary Hanson, Bellevue, Washington; photograph by Beverly Rush)

adds no thickness to the waistline. The covered buttons, loops, and lining are all of the same dull-finish satin. The inside is complete with wide brocade ribbon on the band and herringbone stitch along the edge to fasten the lining. It is an excellent example of total design.

The large thread-covered hooks and eyes usually used on furs look fine for fasteners—not hidden, but right on top. They come in limited colors: black, brown, and some neutrals.

The simple device of two buttons and one cord is a closure easily done or undone. Sew a button on each edge of an opening; crochet chain a cord circle; loop around one button, then twist into a figure eight and loop around the opposite button. Another way is to crochet two smaller circles and put one over each button (catch down under the button with a few stitches so it doesn't come off). To close, each cord loop crosses over to the other button. Pairs of buttons act as lacing hooks. The cord is caught around the buttons—crossing, encircling, and crossing—much like the hooks at the top of heavy boots (also, something like the beads and cords in figure 5-15).

The neckpiece of knitted cords in assorted yarns and colors, shown in figure 4-5, could be adapted for a belt, with cords slipped through a wooden slide from opposite directions (like the shell in figure 5-3); or through two slides

with ends tied to fasten; or any number of other variations. Knit several cords in different yarn textures and colors, tie all of them around your waist. The ends could be festooned with tassels or beads.

Shop the hardware, drapery, notion, and sewing counters for curtain rings of metal or wood or small plastic or metal rings and in tack shops for objects to use in different ways. The round metal bridle buttons with two long center slits seen in figure 5-2 are found in tack shops and are part of a horse bridle; when you require a large, showy button, these are ideal. The long slits accommodate thongs or cords. The loop or buttonhole to surround one has to be very large, so two other ways to close them were devised: a cord or thong is fastened to one edge, a button on the other, then the cord is wrapped across around the button (much like figure 5-18); or, leave long ends on the thongs or yarn fastening the buttons to the cloth, take them out of the center, and tie to close.

Horseshoe nails (new ones!) are fine for picks in pick, button, and cord closures. Small eyelets or slits could be worked right in the cloth and the nails pinned through. Pewter buttons would harmonize with the silver-colored metal of the nails. The cord, pick, button, and bar idea, shown in figure 5-1, is basic, with almost endless possibilities and combinations of materials. I have used teak cocktail picks, slim bones, golf tees, tiny demitasse spoons, as well as tapestry bobbins and large-size blunt end needles! Don't be afraid of a little whimsy here—they are removable and easily changed and replaced. It's fun to hunt and discover new ones!

5-22. A clever cord and button arrangement, where a cord is sewn to each side of the opening. On one side, a large-hole button is slipped onto the cord; on the other side, the cord is pulled through the button in a loop. To fasten, the loop is put over the opposite button and the loop-cord pulled to draw the edges together. (On a wool coat by Jan Burhen)

Buttons and Such

It is worthwhile to have special handcrafted buttons made of wood, enamelled copper, ceramics, metals—and treat them like family jewels! Following are some of mine that are old faithfuls.

Three sets of walnut-wood buttons made for me over thirty years ago have been moved from garment to garment dozens of times. Perfectly plain squares in two sizes (the largest square is on the second band, figure 5-2) and rectangular ones feature the beauty of the wood and have enhanced woven tweeds and knitted coats. Small silver circles, in two sizes, made for me by weaver Kit Gifford, are becoming classics, and already have been used in three different ways (figures 4-49 and 5-14). Small silver and copper buttons as finely crafted as jewelry, which I found on a Mexican shirt, will be saved and used many times. Delicately painted Satsuma ceramic buttons from Japan have served on several garments. A set of Chinese silk knotted buttons and loops, cut from an ancient, worn Chinese robe, now grace a padded jacket. Cord frogs of intricate knotted patterns and an assortment of colors make encore appearances as hair-holders or closures. Cut steel buttons that ornamented a costume in the 1800s have so far been used on two handwoven dresses

and a cardigan. Recently acquired small bits of intricate Chinese embroidery from old robes will become part of closures and trim on silk.

And so on! Looking for appropriate closures is absorbing and they are easily carried souvenirs of travel. Look over your own treasures—an heirloom clasp or set of buttons may be the inspiration for a whole costume designed around them. (I

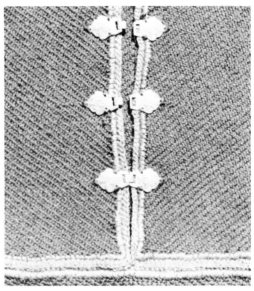

5-23. The subtle sheen of pewter clasps complement the muted colors of Jean Sullivan's slipover top.

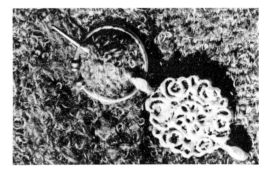

5-24. The fibula or brooch fastener dates back to the Vikings, who flung animal skins around their shoulders, stabbing huge swordlike pins through to fasten them. The sharp metal pin is part of an ornate medallion, which is hinged or has a movable separate ring with an open space. The pin is inserted into the cloth and the ring is moved around to lock it in. My quite old fibula is small, but a realistic size for my handwoven coat.

am sure you wouldn't put shiny, bright plastic buttons on your handspun, handwoven garment of subtle, specially dyed colors, or pin on a gaudy rhinestone bauble.) It has been very re-assuring the last few years to see the appropriate closures, trims, and finishing touches appearing as more and more weavers understand and venture into a completely designed product. This chapter reads like a catalogue of miscellaneous findings for fabricators—and maybe it is! Imaginative but suitable solutions to prosaic buttoning-up are fun and exciting.

SIGNATURES

As designers and craftsmen, we have some ideas and methods that become uniquely our own—our signatures. My all-time favorites for closures or trims are the fascinating little clay spindle

5-25. My signature—ancient spindle whorls used in many ways. This necklace was made for a tussah silk dress (in the background). A sinnet of the same silk was knotted, a jade ring added, then a large spindle whorl from Peru became the top of the tassel. The ends are small tassels with very small spindle whorls as crowns.

whorls from drop spindles used in Peru, Africa, and Mexico (some are shown in figures 5-1 and 5-8). Most have an incised design that is either geometric or of whimsical little figures. I have some with monkeys, pelicans, and other mystic creatures. Part of their charm is the care and love put into ornamenting a tool, even carving a pair of tiny animals on a half-inch clay whorl. There are numerous forms and sizes: round, peaked, flattened, cone-shape, or oval. The hole in the center for the little wooden stick spindle makes them perfect endings for cord or thong ties; or as the tops of tassels (figure 5-25). A small collection of them is suspended by leather thongs from a necklace of potshard beads. The thong suggests the drop spindle. Worn often, in many ways, these small appropriate treasures have become a signature for this handweaver!

Remember that the small finishing touches relfect the interests, taste, and expertise of the weaver or embroiderer. Let your signatures be appropriate and carefully handcrafted or selected.

There is so much more I want to share with you! Teaching this extensive subject in workshops and slide-lectures all over our country and in Canada for many years has been so rewarding. The deep interest, sharing, and expertise of weavers and embroiderers has brought me many fresh ideas and clever solutions to finishing handwovens. It has been difficult to compress and cut, but I hope you will find a fund of information and methods, and that those I promised are in, too! There is always more!

IN CLOSING

This book has developed into a very personal interpretation of the scores of techniques, methods, and ideas for crafting the final finishing, the hallmark of an artist-craftsman. My files bulge with notes and quick sketches from years of studying textiles and costumes. Publications from obscure journals to modern books, and my own previous books, have helped to set the style of bringing this information together in one book. Teaching and talking with textile artists throughout the country, I sensed there was a further need for guidance in planning and creating completely finished products, as an artisan should. Sharing is the appropriate use of knowledge and experience gained, and I happily share with you.

Bibliography/Sources

Joinings, Edges, and Trims is a culmination of my continuous study, research, and experimentation with stitches, weaving techniques, costumes, and textiles; of the publication of many books; and of workshops and slide lectures throughout the United States and Canada. Books are just a small part of the sources contributing to the knowledge of weaving and related crafts. Museum and gallery collections, special exhibits, the incredible number of presentations, studies, and workshops provided by weaving and embroidery guilds, and private collections are all places to look for inspiration. A few of the good, standard references that have served me so well, especially for this subject, follow. Although some of them are out of print, they are well worth the search in your libraries.

Books

Baizerman, Suzanne and Searle, Karen. *Finishes in the Ethnic Tradition*. St. Paul, Minn.: Dos Tejedoras, 1978

Bennet, D.J. *Machine Embroidery with Style*. Connecting Thread Series. Seattle: Madrona Publishers, Inc., 1980

Cone, Ferne Geller. *Knit with Style*. Connecting Thread Series. Seattle: Madrona Publishers, Inc., 1979

Cordry, Donald and Dorothy. *Mexican Indian Costumes*. Austin and London: University of Texas Press, 1968

deDillmont, Therese. *Encyclopedia of Needlework*. Mulhouse, France: D.M.C. Library

D'Harcourt, Raoul. *Textiles of Ancient Peru and Their Techniques*. Translated by Sadie Brown; edited by Grace G. Denny and Carolyn Osborn. Seattle: University of Washington Press, 1962

Drooker, Penelope B. *Embroidering with the Loom*. New York: Van Nostrand Reinhold Co., 1979

Emory, Irene. *The Primary Structure of Fabrics: An Illustrated Classification*. Washington, D.C.: The Textile Museum, 1966

Enthoven, Jacqueline. *The Stitches of Creative Embroidery*. New York: Van Nostrand Reinhold Co., 1964

Hoover, Doris and Welch, Nancy. *Tassels*. Palo Alto, Ca.: Apple Tree Lane, 1978

Nordfors, Jill. *Needle Lace and Needleweaving*. New York: Van Nostrand Reinhold Co., 1974

Rush, Beverly. *Stitch with Style*. Connecting Thread Series. Seattle: Madrona Publishers, Inc., 1979

Tacker, Harold and Sylvia. *Band Weaving*. New York: Van Nostrand Reinhold Co., 1974

Tilke, Max. *Costume Patterns and Designs*. Reprint. New York: Hastings House Publishers, 1974. This book was first printed in 1945 as a supplement to earlier titles on the history of costume. It is a survey of costume patterns and designs of all periods and nations—from antiquity to modern times—and is a springboard for the study of shapes and embellishments.

Wilson, Jean. *Jean Wilson's Soumak Workbook*. Loveland, Colo.: Interweave Press, 1982

————. *The Pile Weaves*. Van Nostrand Reinhold Co., 1974 (revised edition published by Charles Scribner's Sons, 1979)

————. *Weaving Is for Anyone*. New York: Van Nostrand Reinhold Co., 1967

————. *Weaving Is Creative: A Guide to the Weaver Controlled Weaves*. New York: Van Nostrand Reinhold Co., 1972

————. *Weaving Is Fun*. New York: Van Nostrand Reinhold Co., 1971

————. *Weave with Style*. Seattle: Madrona Publishers, Inc., 1979

————. *Weaving You Can Use*. New York: Van Nostrand Reinhold Co., 1975

————. *Weaving You Can Wear*. New York: Van Nostrand Reinhold Co., 1973

Periodicals

These not only present stimulating ideas, but also offer book reviews to keep you up-to-date on new books.

Handwoven. Interweave Press, Loveland, Colorado

The Flying Needle. Membership magazine of the National Standards Council of American Embroiderers

Shuttle, Spindle and Dyepot. Membership magazine of the Handweavers Guild of America

The Weaver's Journal. Boulder, Colorado

Index

Italics indicate illustrations.

African tunic, joins and edges sampler, *59*, 68–71
Albiston, Pat, velvet patchwork caftan made by, 97
Algerian eye stitch, 124
Ancient stitch, 66
Antique stitch, 66
Antwerp edging stitch, 74
Applied fringe, 109
Arrowhead tacks, 98–99
Asian robe, decorative hem of, 52

Bands, woven, 32
   decorative, woven-on, 27–28
   fringed, 109, 112
   as joins, 92
   as tabs, 50
Bar with chain joining stitch, 90
Bars, horizontal, 136
Basket edge stitch, 34–35
Basket stitch, as joining stitch, 82
Baskets, design ideas from, 24, 58
Beaded fringes, 107
Beads, as loops, *134*
Bindings, 32–34
   lace, 56
   stitches for, 34–37
Blanket stitch variations, *15*, 16, *34*, 71–74
Blind hemming, 58
Bobbins, closures from, 137
"Bonus" stitches, 82–83
Bookmark, Greek, 57
Braided warp ends, 104, 105
Broach fastener, *139*
Burhen, Jan, woven-on facings by, 30
Burial ornaments, 122–123
Butted seams, 64
Buttonhole stitches, 14, *15, 54, 69, 70,* 71–74
Buttonholes, slit-weave, 132–134
Buttons, 127–128, 138
   handmade, 139
   woven in, 129

Caftan, patchwork, 97
Camel saddlebags, 132–134
Carr, Pat, cap and scarf made by, 93
Chain stitch, *34, 77*
   over buttonhole stitch, 74, *75*

Chenille, 29, 37
   warps wrapped with, 12, *13*
Chevron stitch, 85–86, *89*
Child's jacket, Greek, 96
Chinese silk purse, *20, 34,* 123
Chinese tassels, *113, 118*
Christmas ornaments, tassels as, *114*
Closed Cretan stitch, 76
Closed herringbone stitch, 81
Closures, 8, 14, *15,* 126–140
Coca bags, 36, *121*
Collected edge, 43–44
Columns, 48, 50–51
Cord closures, 133–135
Cord-and-pick closures, 136
Cords, knitted, 32–33
Creative Stitches of Embroidery, Enthoven, 35
Cretan stitch, 76, 82
Crochet, 37
Crochet joins, 95–96
Crocheted loops, 131
Cuff, knitted, 38
Czech edge, warp and finish, 43, 49, *105*

Damascus edge, 47
Darned-in warp ends, 40
Design, 5, 8–9, 21
   of joins, 61–64
   of selvedges, 24–25
Double selvedge, *15,* 16, 26–27
Dovetail join, 27
Drawn-thread border, 55
Drawn-up weft, for skirt waistband, 57, *137*

Edge tapes, Peruvian, undulating, 28–29
Edges, 21
   applied, 32
   sampler of, *15,* 16
Embellishment, 7, 21, *59,* 122–125
   See also Trim
Embroidery stitches, 67
   sampler of, 16–19
   in selvedge, 22
   See also name of stitch
Ends, 21
Enthoven, Jacqueline, *Creative Stitches of Embroidery,* 35
Eskimo lacing edge stitch, *18,* 35–36, *69, 70*

DATE			